THE EMPATH'S SURVIVAL GUIDE

SIMPLE AND EFFECTIVE PRACTICES TO
BECOME AN ENERGY HEALER AND
DEVELOP YOUR MYSTIC CONSCIOUSNESS

(EMPATH RISING 2.0)

GLENN CUMMINGS

TABLE OF CONTENTS

Introduction

Congratulations on purchasing this copy of *Empath Healing: The Empath's Survival Guide. Simple And Effective Practices To Become An Energy Healer And Develop Your Mystic Consciousness* and thank you for doing so. Within the following chapters, you'll find a comprehensive guide for empaths of any type, or any level of experience, to channel their empathic gifts into healing. While we will touch briefly on definitions of empathy and the common experiences of those who identify as empaths within the first few chapters, this book will be primarily focused on the process of healing the self and others with your empathic sensibilities. It will be geared towards those readers who have already self-identified as empaths, and are now wondering:

"What comes next?"

"How can I manage my empathic abilities, instead of allowing them to manage me?"

"Will these feelings ever change?"

"Why am I like this?

"Why does everyone else seem to see the world so differently from the way I see (or feel, or know) things?"

"Will things get better for me, with time? Or will they get worse?"

"Does it ever get easier?"

"How can I protect myself?"

"How do I hold onto my strength, energy levels, positivity, and joy in the face of adversity?"

"Now that I've discovered this ability... what am I supposed to *do* with it?"

This being the case, it may be helpful for those who are new to the concept of empathic sensitivity to further research any terms or ideas mentioned in the first three chapters that are mainly foreign, novel, or confusing to them, before reading on.

This book will also be helpful to those who recognize a loved one as empathic and wish to understand their particular challenges and strengths better, or perhaps offer guidance and support to an empath who appears to be struggling. It must be said, however, that an essential step in an empath's journey is learning self-determination; therefore, it is always preferable for developing empaths to read a text like this for themselves, rather than having the information relayed through a third party as advice. Many empaths who have not yet fully empowered themselves will struggle to differentiate between their own feelings and desires, and the emotions and motivations that other people *expect* them to own. Even those who are well-intentioned and full of love for the empath may inadvertently superimpose their own values, beliefs, and judgments into their interpretation of this text, and therefore serve to distort the empath's understanding of these concepts.

By contrast, when an empath is able to read through this book on their own, they'll be far more likely to connect on a personal level and identify the specific emotional experiences that resonate most with them. All empaths have a few things in common, but there is a great deal of diversity within the empath community, as well. Some advice for empaths can be designed from a one-size-fits-all perspective, but not all; physical empaths, for example, may find their healing journey follows quite a different path than that of an emotional or geomantic empath. Likewise, an empowered empath may take a different message away from this book than a repressed, unconscious, or broken empath would. Age, gender identity, race, sexual orientation, personality, profession, and background experience all work in concert to define any empath's perspective on the world around them and their internal landscape. It is crucial for every empath to recognize that they are not alone in their struggles, but that they are each unique and precious as a rare gem. Doing so will allow the empath to overcome the challenges of their sensitivities, rather than viewing them as a shortcoming or curse, and embrace their abilities, looking at them not only as a gift but as a superpower that they would be remiss in keeping hidden away from the rest of the world.

Many empaths carry deep emotional wounds. Often, we are taught from a young age that our sensitivities are unacceptable—that we must hide them, or learn to outgrow them, and disguise our true natures in order to fit in and thrive in an empathy-deficient world. But empaths are natural healers, truth-tellers, emotional and spiritual beacons. The ultimate goal of this book will be to rewrite the story that empaths have been told about themselves by others, in order to help them see their inherent value and reach their full potential. If you have been told throughout your life that you are too sensitive, too intense, too emotional, or just generally *too much*, you may have grown to view your empathic abilities as a fire inside you that needs to be stomped out. My hope is that by the time you finish this book, you'll instead see that fire as one that should be fed because it is a rare point of light in a vast sea of darkness. The world needs you and the fire you carry inside. When you learn to heal yourself, your fire will grow and shine bright; when you learn to heal others, that fire will catch, and your light will spread throughout the world.

There are plenty of books available on this subject, so thank you again for choosing this one. Every effort was made to ensure it is full of as much useful information as possible. Please enjoy!

- Chapter 1 -

WHAT IS AN EMPATH?

In order to understand why empaths are so well suited to the healing arts, we must first look at their most common characteristics, and examine the ways in which the empath typically differs from the average individual. We'll also clarify the definition of empathy as a fluid, rather than fixed, trait, which can be both good and bad, rather than the exemplary moral virtue it is often believed to be.

THE EMPATHY SCALE

Many of us fall into the habit of describing empathy as a personality trait that people either have in spades or lack entirely. It does simplify things when we look at the personalities of others as innate, fixed, and predictable, allowing us to praise and embrace those we think of as warm and giving, while we can write off those we see as callous or self-absorbed.

In truth, though, empathy is one of several "traits" that would be better described as "skills." While the scientific analysis does show evidence that some degree of empathetic capacity stems from genetic inheritance, there is far more evidence to show that empathy is either fostered or repressed experientially in most individuals. Empathy is not something you are born with or born without—instead, it is a coping mechanism that most all of us rely on in early life. Our childhood surroundings will often determine the extent to which we continue to rely on empathy for survival, as we grow to adulthood, or learn to loosen its grip on our emotional and physical bodies so that we can function as individuals.

Most people learn, as they mature, to fall somewhere in the middle of the empathy scale; from this position, they are able to connect empathetically with those they love, or sometimes with strangers, when they have the capacity and strength to do so, while disconnecting from their empathic impulses when it makes more sense to focus on their own feelings and needs. These people are able to give to charities without bankrupting themselves; they are also able to support their friends emotionally, but avoid those who are suffering when they need to focus on their own emotional pain. This is considered the "normal" range of empathy.

Things work differently on the far ends of the empathy scale, though. Some of us may learn to detach from our empathetic impulses entirely, developing empathy-deficient personality disorders (such as antisocial personality disorder or narcissistic personality disorder, among others); meanwhile, there are some who grow up in environments that never train them to manage their empathetic impulses, whose emotional behavior might be described as "hyper-empathetic." Those who are empathy-deficient will often present as self-absorbed, inconsiderate, greedy or stingy, and uncaring; they might never feel compelled to donate a penny to charity, despite having more money than they could ever feasibly spend in their own lifetime. Meanwhile, empaths, or hyper-empathetic people, tend to be far more focused on others than on themselves; they can be overly generous, highly sensitive, deeply affectionate, compassionate, and selfless, often to a fault.

The impulse to empathize with others may be naturally stronger in some people than others, but regardless of the person's background and current persona, their empathetic capacity can always be enhanced, or grow more inaccessible through lack of use. Empathy is quite a bit like muscle mass; anyone can lose their empathetic strength through prolonged emotional laziness or by embracing a defensive mindset, but at the same time, there's nothing to stop even the leanest and weakest among us from growing strong and powerful, so long as they are willing to do some hard, transformative work and break their counterproductive habits.

EMPATHY AND SYMPATHY

The concept of empathy is often described as something interchangeable with sympathy, but in reality, the two words describe vastly different internal thought processes. Sympathy is a theoretical emotive response and one which is generally chosen rather than experienced involuntarily. Usually, even if we aren't conscious of the thought process, we decide whether or not others are deserving of our sympathy before we allow ourselves to be emotionally moved. This is perhaps why so many of the homeless who sustain themselves on spare change feel the need to hold signs that explain how they came to find themselves in such a position, or remind others of their own humanity and victimization; without these props to elicit sympathy, many passers-by would presume this person to be a criminal or a hopeless addict, and excuse themselves from the act of sympathizing, choosing to ignore or even antagonize them based on a split-second judgment.

When we see or hear about another person's suffering, we often express our sympathy by saying something along the lines of: "I feel bad for this individual." Usually, what we mean by this is actually closer to the following sentiment: "I understand this individual's suffering on a theoretical level, and I *would* feel very badly *if* I were standing in their shoes."

Empathy, by contrast, removes the hypothetical aspect of this thought process, closing the cognitive distance between the sufferer and the compassionate observer. For many people, empathy also removes the aspect of choice. When we empathize with someone else, we don't just imagine that we *would* feel bad *if* we were in their position; instead of feeling bad *for* another person, we feel badly right along *with* them, and the emotional responses they stir up within us are often overwhelming, involuntary, and difficult to shake. We experience another person's pain, sorrow, anger, excitement, fear, humiliation, joy, or confusion, as though it were our own emotional burden to carry.

Whereas many people infer a connotation to negative emotions when they think of sympathy, empathy can allow us to experience the full range of emotional, and sometimes physical, responses, whether positive, negative, or somewhere in between, as we detect these sensations in others. Think of a wedding guest who is moved to tears of joy while watching the ceremony; this person most likely isn't crying because they feel sad, nor because they feel a sense of sympathy for the couple, but rather because they are able to empathize with the couple and other members of the wedding party, overwhelmed by all of the powerful emotional energies flowing through the room. This type of empathetic response can also apply to emotional sensations that are more confusing or difficult to name; for instance, a highly empathetic person might feel an unsettling mix of unrecognizable emotions in an environment full of cognitive dissonance, or when surrounded by liars. As compared to sympathy, empathy is a far more immediate, compulsive, and multidimensional experience. There is usually a limit to how much sympathy we can feel or express for another person; however, with empathy, the potential for depth and breadth of emotional connection is boundless.

THE SCIENCE OF EMPATHY

Empaths and empath healers are more widely recognized and appreciated outside the realms of western medicine and science. Some skeptics balk at the term "empath" and question the existence of such an identity, believing it to be synonymous with the supernatural and metaphysical only, rather than something rooted in reality. Some are unwilling to believe anything they cannot see proven in scientifically measurable terms.

These naysayers might be surprised to learn that there is a great deal of scientific evidence to support not only the existence of measurable empathetic responses in most humans, but also the existence of hyper-empathetic individuals, or empaths.

There is no question that empathy itself is as real as rock, both demonstrable and measurable. Each of us is gifted with a mirror-neuron system (though it is more active in some than others) that allows us to connect to the observed experiences of others. This is most likely an evolutionary tool to promote self-preservation, as it causes us to be more alert and attentive when we see another person in danger or pain and take steps to avoid repeating their fate. The mirror-neuron system also helps us to feel happy when we see others having fun or to feel hungry when we see others eating a hearty meal. It is also why sad movies can move us to tears and why pornography has the power to excite us sexually. Mirror-neurons often inspires involuntary and subconscious reactions; we yawn when we see someone else yawning, and automatically smile or scowl to reflect the facial expression of anyone addressing us. We even feel the impulse to mimic foreign accents after just a few minutes of conversation with someone whose speech pattern differs from our own.

It is a scientific fact—not metaphysical theory—that our physical actions impact our emotions and thoughts. A sad person who holds a pencil in between their teeth can quickly trick their own brain into believing that they have something to smile about; if a smile is inspired, instead, by the sight of someone else smiling, the emotional impact is the same. Our mirror-neurons can literally make emotions contagious, pushing us to feel the same way as the people around us do.

Furthermore, it has been scientifically proven that a small percentage of the population possesses overactive mirror-neuron systems. These people mimic even the subtlest of behavioral shifts, and their impulse to mirror observed behavior is both immediate and overpowering. While the term "empath" may not garner much respect or acceptance in the world of science, evidence to support the existence of empaths is irrefutable.

The Evolutionary Purpose of Empathy

Empathy is easily observable in most infants and young children. Infants in neonatal wards will most often exhibit contagious crying; one baby will begin to wail over genuine discomfort, but the surrounding children will most often join in soon thereafter, unable to distinguish between their own emotions and the pain of others. As they grow into toddlerhood, most children will continue to exhibit involuntary empathy, mirroring the facial expressions of the adults in their lives, even without understanding the motivations behind these emotions. Children need to be hyper-empathetic during these developmental stages; this is how they learn to interact with other humans, even before they are able to speak.

Most often, as children continue to grow and begin to grasp the language as a communicative tool, they will still experience contagious crying, infectious laughter, and other emotional states as though they are viral. However, during these developmental years, children raised in healthy and supportive environments will also begin to learn to differentiate their own emotions, physical feelings, and needs from those that rightfully belong to other people. This is the stage at which most children learn to advocate for themselves. Depending on how their empathetic or self-serving behaviors are received, they will eventually settle into a style of empathetic connection (or lack thereof) that allows them to feel safe and accepted. A child raised in a chaotic or volatile environment may detach from their empathic impulses in order to protect themselves; meanwhile, an only child of an emotionally repressed parent may develop hyper-empathy so that they can still feel their parent's love, even when it isn't expressed.

It seems that almost every position on the empathy scale, no matter how healthy or destructive it may appear, is valuable to the function of society at large—even those who are so deficient in empathy as to become violent. Those who are highly empathic tend to be community-minded, focused on what serves and protects everyone; those who are empathy-deficient, by contrast, are more likely to focus on the single-minded pursuit of their personal goals. Together, these types create a balance between thought and action, practicality and emotionality, forward momentum and retrospection. The empath tends to be more open-minded, tolerant, and giving, while those who are empathy-deficient are often defensive, judgmental, and focused on self-preservation above all else. When it comes to managing resources and establishing cultural values, there is a place for both points of view within any community.

EMPATHY VS. EMPATHIC SENSITIVITY

Many people suffer from the misconception that empaths are defined simply as people who are capable of feeling and expressing empathy; in truth, though, everyone is capable of accessing empathy, even malignant narcissists. The trick is to evaluate whether or not that empathy is voluntary. A malignant narcissist may sometimes choose to exercise their empathetic muscle as a means to manipulate others, or to endear themselves to a strategic target. A person who falls in the "normal" empathetic range will most likely feel involuntarily compelled to empathize with those they love or those who remind them of themselves. Meanwhile, a true empath is often unable to discriminate in this arena; they compulsively empathize with loved ones and strangers alike, with both victims and aggressors, even sometimes with people who have caused the empath direct and purposeful harm.

Most people automatically work to distance themselves from empathetic connections that are unpleasant or seem potentially dangerous. Empaths, meanwhile, are usually only able to do this through extensive training. Furthermore, people who fall into the normal range of empathy learn to notice that which is relevant to their experience and ignore that which is not—they can pass a crying stranger on the street without giving them a second thought, but when their best friend is in tears, they become hyper-alert and observative. Those who are empathy-deficient generally only take note of things that impact them directly, so they aren't likely to care much about anyone's tears except their own. By contrast, a true empath will often give equal emotional and mental weight to everything they take note of; to them, there is no difference between the tears of a stranger on the street, tears falling from their best friend's eyes, tears that fall on the opposite side of the planet, and tears that stream down their own cheeks.

Common Traits of an Empath

The empath community is home to a cast of unique characters; that being said, there are a number of common traits that empaths of all types tend to exhibit. Here is a list of just a few of those traits. There are many, many more, which I invite you to discover by reaching out to other empaths and sharing your experiences.

Empaths tend to be...

- Extremely sensitive, both emotionally and physically
- Introverted, or easily overwhelmed by a lack of privacy or alone time
- Creative minded and expressive
- Overly generous
- Diplomatic
- Detail-oriented
- Sometimes absent-minded or forgetful
- Peacemakers

- Picky about the things they consume (from food to television, to the energy source that fuels their home or car)
- Chronically fatigued
- People pleasers
- Free spirits and wanderers
- Frequently suffering from lower back pain and indigestion.
- Nature lovers and animal enthusiasts
- Surrounded by people who rely on their support, advice, guidance, and compassion.
- Quiet and reserved
- Deep thinkers

THE EMPATH AND THE HIGHLY SENSITIVE PERSON

While the empathic identity may still be viewed as a fringe concept by some in the fields of psychology and social work, Highly Sensitive People, or HSPs, are commonly recognized within both fields. Some literature may refer to empaths and HSPs interchangeably, equating the two identities; while they have a great deal in common, there are some noted differences between a Highly Sensitive Person and an empath. The chances are that most empaths are also HSPs (but not all); conversely, there are likely many Highly Sensitive People who are not especially empathetic or empathic.

The primary difference seems to lie in the way each identity processes their emotional responses to information. Both HSPs and empaths are more likely than others to notice minor details and small behavioral shifts in other people; both have a tendency to feel emotions more deeply than others and to pick up on energies that aren't their own.

Yet the Highly Sensitive Person generally seems able to differentiate between the emotions and physical sensations that should rightfully be their own, and those of others; in fact, some report that emotional contagion from others often feels physically invasive or threatening, and inspires a visceral reaction that prompts them to strictly enforce their boundaries and distance themselves from any energy source that feels overwhelming. Some HSPs can actually grow quite detached from their empathetic impulses, using impassivity as a shield and emotional isolation as a survival mechanism. Their heightened sensitivity does not necessarily inspire them to share in the emotions they detect in others; they may present as more judgmental than compassionate and understanding (though this is not always the case).

Empaths, by contrast, will always struggle to remain unaffected by external energies unless they take specific precautions to keep themselves balanced, guarded, and consistently replenished. They often feel that their connections to others are obligatory and that they do not have a choice in the matter.

Though different studies and sources tend to report varied numbers, it is generally believed that only about one or two percent of the population could be diagnosed as hyper-empathetic or empathic. Meanwhile, it is estimated that as much as twenty percent of the population might identify as highly sensitive. It is possible that HSPs are repressed or disempowered empaths, and that most could be trained to enhance their sensitivities to the level of empathic power with the right guidance and support from experienced empaths.

- Chapter 2 -

THE EMPATH'S DILEMMA

Many discussions of empathy outside of the worlds of psychology or social science are based upon the oversimplified premise that empathy is always good—that it is, in fact, the highest of moral virtues, and that its power can heal all wounds, stop conflict in its tracks, combat hatred and replace it with peace, love, and harmony.

Make no mistake, reader—your author believes wholeheartedly that empathy is indeed one of the most powerful and effective tools on the planet for fostering positivity, emotional health, and social harmony. However, like most powerful tools, it can become ineffective, or even dangerous, when used incorrectly, by an inexperienced or ill-intentioned hand. Like fire, empathy can provide warmth, light, and energy, but it can also quickly become a destructive force when used carelessly. In order to harness its power for good, we must understand empathy thoroughly, which means examining both its good and bad sides unflinchingly.

EMPATHY: A DOUBLE-EDGED SWORD

Empathy is a powerful force that should be used mindfully. When we empathize with others, we feel strong connections with everything that informs their world views. We don't only take on their joy or pain—we may sometimes absorb their anger, shame, self-doubt, or hatred of others. This can be dangerous for empaths, who may unconsciously amplify these feelings within themselves to the point of harboring toxic anger that isn't even theirs to own. Furthermore, empaths may over-empathize with those who have been victimized, and therefore detach from the ability to empathize with anyone that the victim blames for their suffering; alternatively, if the empath maintains empathetic connections with both the victim and the aggressor in any situation, the cognitive dissonance this creates can manifest in unpleasant physical symptoms, causing headaches or stomach pains, intense anxiety, or the sensation of being physically pulled in two different directions, emotionally torn in half.

When we empathize too strongly with any one person or group, we generally lose the ability to empathize with their opposites. A person who over-empathizes with women as victims of a patriarchal society, for existence, may begin to lose sight of the fact that men are human, and that, while some may be misogynists, others may be blameless, well-intentioned feminists. Too much empathy within a secluded group can encourage members to view all outsiders as inhuman; this was often the case in ancient societies, who falsely claimed that members of other groups were cannibalistic and used this misinformation to justify waging wars or usurping their resources.

Even outside of a group setting, empaths must remain mindful of the potential for empathy to become dangerous, or detrimental to their own well-being. In one-on-one relationships, empaths tend to over-identify with the feelings of others over their own, meaning they often forgive too easily and grow to view the emotions of others as objectively more important than their own. If an empath is involved in a relationship with someone who hurts them, emotionally or physically, they run the risk of internalizing whatever emotions or thoughts this person uses to justify the harm they've caused. This can result in self-doubt, self-hatred, and in some extreme cases, self-harm.

THE EMPATH'S ARCH NEMESIS

Empaths are found on the far end of the empathy scale, experiencing empathetic connections more frequently than the majority of the population. On the opposite end of the empathy scale, we find those who suffer from a variety of empathy-deficient disorders. Some of these are medical or mental disorders, in which the lack of empathy displayed by the patient in question does not necessarily imply any sort of nefarious intentions or malicious attitude towards others; people on the autism spectrum, for example, may struggle to display compassionate attitudes or mirror the emotions of those around them, while still harboring nothing but the best of intentions towards humanity at large. In these disorders, some professionals believe that the lack of empathy displayed is merely a reflection of an inability to interpret the emotional signals of other people; if these patients can learn to decode social cues and understand the impact of their own reactions, they are often willing to adjust their behaviors accordingly. They don't object to interpersonal harmony but tend to view the world, by default, through a self-centered lens.

Meanwhile, there are some who suffer from empathy-deficient disorders that can make them quite dangerous. Narcissists, in particular, can pose a great threat to empaths, especially those who have not yet awakened to the full extent of their empathic power. Narcissism is a personality disorder wherein a person is capable of theoretical empathy and feigned sympathy, meaning that they *do* understand social cues and emotional signals, and can theoretically place themselves in another's shoes; however, the narcissist most often chooses to exploit this knowledge and use it to manipulate others, rather than choosing to empathize with them.

They consistently choose to put their own needs ahead of everyone else's, regardless of circumstance, and subordinate others in order to feed their own egos, addicted to the feeling of superiority.

Some believe that empaths and narcissists are cosmically linked. They are often drawn to each other in romantic, platonic, and even professional relationships (though their relationships are usually toxic, to some degree), and many empaths credit the narcissists in their lives with the discovery of their empathic abilities, claiming that through their emotional abuse, the narcissist inspired them to rediscover their authentic self and pursue personal growth. Some even credit narcissists with the very *existence* of the empathic gift, suggesting that narcissistic abuse trains its victims to become hyper-sensitive, intuitive, and compassionate for the sake of self-protection.

The trouble, though, lies in the very nature of narcissistic abuse, which is a byproduct of the personality disorder, rather than a form of purposeful destruction. Narcissists generally train those around them not only accept their behavior, but to normalize, idealize, and even mimic it. Think, for example, of a dinner party with six guests, where the host has prepared six chicken breasts, one for each guest. If one guest is a narcissist, they might saunter up to the table before being invited to, and help themselves to two or more of those chicken breasts, with no regard for the fact that this will leave another guest with an empty plate. If you, as another guest, have spent a great deal of time around this narcissist, and are used their self-serving behavior, you will likely have learned that if you want to eat, you'll have to follow their lead; otherwise, you'll be the one who goes hungry. Even if justice and generosity are deeply embedded in your personal nature, narcissistic abuse will train you to look at the world through a mindset of scarcity and self-defense, even when there is abundance and no real threat to your well-being.

Empaths must learn how to recognize narcissists and their abusive behaviors as early as possible, to avoid becoming intimately involved or reliant upon them in relationships. For the empath, especially, narcissistic abuse can function as a mental cage with a downward spiral. The abuse encourages the empath to suppress their natural empathetic instincts, and teaches them to behave as though they are narcissists themselves around everyone else (save the abuser in their lives)—this makes it extremely difficult for them to seek out help, to trust in their own instincts and inherent goodness, and to maintain faith in the karmic balance of the universe.

THE PERSECUTION WOUND

Most empaths have been told myths about their own personalities and abilities from early childhood, many of which are consistently reinforced by the media and members of their communities throughout their lifetimes. Empaths—especially empathic women—have been discredited, invalidated, and villainized for centuries, so those of us who have strong empathic connections can pick up on multiple lifetimes worth of disbelief and negative energy; this means that a single negative or invalidating statement pointed our way can be extraordinarily difficult to brush off, as each statement may carry the weight of hundreds, even thousands, of toxic interactions from the past. This works in much the same way that the utterance of a single racial slur can carry the weight of hundreds of years of institutional injustice.

The persecution wound is a legacy that roots us to the common struggle of empaths throughout history. When someone casually laughs at our claims, calls us frauds or scam artists, or simply sneers at us to convey their disdain for what we do, we are reminded of all the healers throughout Europe and New England who were burned or hanged for witches, made into scapegoats for the irrational fears of others, despite their tireless efforts to heal and help them; we are reminded of all the victims in history who have been blamed for their own victimization; of the many brilliant innovators and scientists who were imprisoned or murdered for daring to see the truth, and share it with those who preferred to remain entrenched in myth. We remember that most of the monumental discoveries and inventions in history were initially reviled, discredited, and punished, rather than embraced or rewarded.

Sometimes, the weight of these collective memories pushes us to silence ourselves, and dim our own energetic glow. It may even inspire us to deny our gifts and repress our true identities. When an empath is stuck in a defensive mindset, encouraged to deny their identity and favor the values of those who discredit them, they may be viewed as a "broken" or "repressed" empath. They will likely direct all of their personal energy into projecting a persona that is entirely oppositional to their authentic self. They will also likely numb themselves to their own cognitive dissonance through addictions of all kinds, putting their authentic minds to sleep and functioning almost as if they were possessed by another spirit. This is a toxic mindset that will often cause even the most naturally empathic people to project negative energy, or "bad vibes," as they are motivated primarily from a sense of fear that they will be discovered for who they really are, and attacked for it.

To become an effective healer, empaths must overcome this challenge and act from a position of self-love, confidence, and self-validation. One way to work on healing your persecution wound and protect yourself from further emotional damage is to recognize the most common myths, decode them, and armor yourself with the ability to translate them into truths. When you understand the root of this mythology, it becomes much easier to prepare yourself for any negation or invalidation that comes your way; furthermore, you'll find it much easier to recognize these false claims for exactly what they are: projected shame, which isn't yours to own, used as a defense mechanism by souls who are trapped in their own anguish and unwilling to self-reflect, heal, or grow.

People who hold all of their pain inside allow it to become a toxic poison inside of them; this manifests as negativity and causes them to feel anger and resentment towards those who are thriving in ways that seem inaccessible to them. As a thriving empath, you will emit an energy of self-awareness, emotional understanding, positivity and progress *through* pain; those who are unwilling to work on self-awareness, those who avoid processing their emotions, and those who allow pain to define and destroy them, will be made uncomfortable by your capabilities, and they will frequently attempt to discredit you. Don't take it personally, and don't accept the myths they try to tell you; decode and rewrite these messages for yourself before you internalize them.

Myth: Empaths are fragile.

Truth: Empaths are extraordinarily strong, resilient, and powerful beings. People who blame empaths for being fragile are generally victim-blaming because it is easier than taking responsibility for causing harm or behaving inappropriately. They are projecting false shame in order to avoid self-reflection.

Myth: Empaths think the whole world revolves around their emotions.

Truth: Empaths know that everything in the universe is energy, including emotions. They don't believe their own emotions require special or extraordinary attention—they believe everyone's feelings deserve to be validated and processed because emotions drive behavior and define our realities.

Myth: Empaths who ask for monetary compensation are con artists, selling make-believe services and encouraging others to believe in things that don't actually exist.

Truth: Many empaths provide healing services to people in their communities for little to no financial compensation. The healing work that empaths provide is often time-consuming, physically and mentally exhausting, and costly. Whether or not you believe that crystals harness metaphysical powers, they cost real money. Time and energy are also worth money. Very few true empaths use their gifts to perpetuate financial abuse or to make inauthentic claims about their own abilities. Most often, they simply wish to offer their gifts to others without being taken advantage of, so that they can continue to maintain their own health and happiness.

Myth: Empaths are delusional and suffering from mental illness.

Truth: The world we live in depends largely on delusion and insanity to function. Empaths are often persecuted for being truth-tellers in communities built upon lies and injustice. They may behave quite differently from most other people, but that does not necessarily mean they are insane. People once believed that Galileo was insane for suggesting the sun was in the center of our solar system. The majority of any population may rule by default, but that does not make it inherently wise or correct.

Chapter 3

EMPATH TYPES

No two empaths are created equal. While most of the available literature on empaths and empath healing tend to focus on the experience of emotional empaths, there are those whose empathetic sensitivity is focused more on physical rather than emotional sensations. There are some who struggle to connect emotionally with most humans, but can easily empathize with animals, plants, or non-living entities, such as places, rocks, or even metaphysical concepts. Some are able to connect with energetic frequencies that are far removed from their present circumstances, rooted in the past, the future, or alternative planes of existence.

Below, we'll explore the most common categorical empath types. As you read, be mindful of the fact that there are always further possibilities; some empaths identify as a combination of two or more types, while some never find a categorical title that seems to fit their specific empathic experience. If you do find that one or more of the type descriptions below strikes a familiar chord, consider this typology as merely a jumping-off point for further research and connection with similar empaths. Don't allow any type to limit your perceptions or belief in your own powers. Many empaths find that their abilities expand and intensify as they age and develop more emotional and spiritual maturity; if you identify as an animal empath now, there is no reason why you might not evolve into an emotional empath at a later point in time. Always keep yourself open to the possibility of growth.

EMOTIONAL EMPATHS

Of all the empath types, emotional empaths are by far the most common. This is perhaps because emotional empathy is a skill most of us already possess in infancy; while many outgrow these strong empathic connections and learn to numb themselves to the emotional energies around them, a fair number of us hold onto this ability in adulthood, and some are even able to train and strengthen their sensitivity to emotional vibrations as they grow older. Some emotional empaths learn to stifle their emotional instincts in adolescence when they begin to learn that others see their sensitivity as a weakness or an annoyance, but most often their empathic gifts will come back to them with an explosive degree of force at some point later in life. Often, emotional empaths rediscover their true identities during the dissolution of a toxic relationship, whether it is familial, professional, platonic, or romantic.

Most emotional empaths feel strong emotional connections to those who are in close proximity to them—strangers they pass by on a walk through the park, for instance—but some are more sensitive to the emotions of people they care for, regardless of how much distance may lay between them. Emotional empaths often pick up on energetic frequencies that vibrate between people, meaning they are able to understand the nuances of others' relationships and detect subtle energetic shifts in group dynamics. They also note tensions between others, however subtle, whether it is sexual tension or the uncomfortable energy created by anger or resentment.

Many emotional empaths can also feel it in their bodies when someone has told a lie, even if the lie wasn't delivered directly to them. As an example, an emotional empath might show up to a birthday party and see a group of friends they haven't interacted with for months; one of the guests at this party has been cheating on their partner, who is also present, for several weeks, and another guest knows about the infidelity, so the two of them have had to tell a number of white lies and greater lies in order to keep this secret under wraps. Even before the empath interacts with either of these people, they are very likely to feel, immediately upon arriving at the party, that something isn't right. They may not know what exactly is causing this negative energy straight away, but as the party continues, they will likely be able to pinpoint where the negative energy is coming from or to sense that the nature of this energy is dishonesty or betrayal.

Empaths are especially sensitive to lies that are told directly to their faces and usually know immediately, down to their bones, when someone has been dishonest with them. This being the case, many emotional empaths have social lives that appear complicated or disjointed to the outside observer. Lies and emotional abuse between other people literally hurt them, so empowered empaths with firm boundaries often know that it's best to walk away from social circles that tolerate or encourage such dynamics. Of all the empath types, emotional empaths are perhaps the most susceptible to narcissistic abuse or exploitation from energy vampires.

EMOTIONAL EMPATHS AS HEALERS

Emotional empaths tend to find their stride as healers of emotional wounds. They are particularly skilled at guiding others through trauma recovery, personal evolution, and release of false psychological complexes. They may also naturally drift into the repair—or dismantling—of unhealthy relationships and toxic cycles, like emotional abuse. Many choose to work as therapists or counselors for individuals, couples, or families, but this work can be quite draining for them. Others may find they are better able to help people through writing, public speaking, or artistic creativity, as these fields allow them to reach a large number of people without leaving themselves constantly vulnerable to emotional contagion, burnout, and compassion fatigue.

Emotional empaths can also apply their skills to the world of medical healing, though this choice is less common. The medical field seldom gives weight to the impact that our emotional bodies can have on our physical ones and vice versa; so, while emotional empaths may be apter than non-empathic medical professionals at untangling complicated diagnoses or understanding the roots of physical pain and other symptoms, their empathic knowledge will usually need to be translated or disguised in some way in order for the empath to be taken seriously. For instance, an emotional empath working as a pediatrician might sense that a child's chronic skin rash has a root in an emotional disturbance—perhaps an authority figure in the child's life is taking advantage of their position and abusing them, either emotionally or physically—but this empath would not be able to tell the child's parents, or their colleagues, that they believe the rash is merely a symptom of holding in a secret that the child thinks of as shameful. They could not send the parents away with a recommended course of radical honesty as a treatment. Their insight may prove quite valuable, but will only be respected if they are able to couch their knowledge within a more widely recognized framework.

Furthermore, emotional empaths can be extraordinarily valuable in the world of physical medicine because they will ensure patients are offered compassion and emotional comfort during treatment. Many doctors lack empathy, at least during work hours, as a way to protect themselves from grief; if they allow themselves to care about their patients, they run the risk of being heartbroken when they are unable to save them from their own mortalities. They aim to care for the patient's body as though it were detached from the soul and mind inside it. By contrast, the emotional empath as a nurse or doctor is far more likely to recognize the importance of good mental and emotional health in any patient's recovery process, and prioritize things like family or friend visits, good nutritional health, books and games to keep the mind active, exposure to sunlight and nature, and so on. They will recognize their patients as whole beings, with a body, mind, and soul all intertwined in such a way that none can function without the other two in balance. They can also have an enormous impact on the lives of those who love their patients, simply by delivering diagnoses or difficult news with compassion in place of impassivity.

PHYSICAL EMPATHS

Physical empaths (also called "medical empaths") are somewhat less common than emotional empaths, though a great number of empaths identify with both types simultaneously. The strictly physical empath is more attuned to the physical experiences of others than their emotional sensations. Some claim they can literally feel the pleasure or pain experienced in another person's body, while others can see or otherwise detect physical disturbances in the energy fields of others. Some might see injuries or illnesses in others' bodies as a color shift in their aura, for example, while some might detect physical ailments through other senses instead, like smell or touch.

PHYSICAL EMPATHS AS HEALERS

Physical empaths are often naturally gifted at hands-on healing practices, such as massage, acupressure, acupuncture, reflexology, chiropractic alignment, yoga instruction, physical therapy, and even traditional western medicine. They have a keen ability to pinpoint the source of another's pain or the root of an illness and can understand physical sensations that patients struggle to describe with language.

The physical empath who chooses to apply their gifts to healing work must stay vigilant in order to protect their own physical body. While they may find they are extraordinarily efficient and talented in whatever healing art they choose, able to secure diagnoses and prescribe treatment much more quickly than their non-empathic counterparts, they may also soon discover that healing work, unfortunately, leaves them quite vulnerable to contracting illnesses and chronic pain disorders themselves. It is not at all uncommon for physical empath healers to report that they experience the full range of painful or uncomfortable sensations that their patients complain of, sometimes retaining these symptoms long after their patients are cured or relieved.

Sadly, physical empaths who suffer from this type of contagion will find it frustrating and difficult to get their own maladies diagnosed or treated by doctors of western medicine, who may infer that their pain or illness is all psychosomatic. It is recommended that physical empath healers rely heavily on their own trusted energy healers to help them maintain metaphysical boundaries, heal imbalances, and untangle their personal bodily feelings from those of their patients and clients. It is also recommended that physical empaths avoid overworking themselves, and aim to work in environments where they can focus on one client at a time without being rushed. A physical empath working in a busy clinic, for instance, or in a chaotic emergency ward, will likely struggle to maintain their energetic boundaries and adequately protect themselves.

SYNESTHETIC EMPATHS

Synesthesia is a fairly rare condition, though it is widely recognized in medical and scientific fields, wherein a person's perceptions of sensory experiences are confused, tangled, or enmeshed. For instance, there are synesthetes who claim to hear colors, feel numerical values, or taste sounds; others might only be able to make sense of the information they see and hear when they have access to both audio and visual stimulus together; some even incorporate extrasensory knowledge, assigning emotional values to things like flavors, colors, or specific notes on the musical scale, perhaps even personifying non-living entities. Not all synesthetes are empaths, but those who are can often access levels of empathic knowledge and sensitivity that mystify the rest of the world, even other powerful and experienced empaths.

Mirror-touch synesthesia is a rare condition to find in the general populace, but it is a particularly common type of synesthesia amongst empaths, in which the visual and tactile cues are mixed up in the brain. An empath with mirror-touch synesthesia could witness another person being pinched on the forearm, and feel pain in their own arm as a result. Likewise, they could witness another person being hugged, and feel the warmth and weight of the embrace throughout their own body.

For most with this condition, it seems that the source of the sensation must be visible in order for the empath to experience the tactile effect. This means that a synesthetic empath would need to actually witness someone else being tickled in order to feel as though they were tickled themselves. Unlike the physical empath, if the synesthetic empath encountered an individual who was writhing on the floor in agony, suffering from an internal, invisible pain, such as a severe stomach ache, they most likely would not feel pain in their own gut; they might, however, feel as though their own limbs were being flailed against the ground as they watch the sufferer rolling about, or perhaps feel the tension in their muscles as they wince and squirm.

SYNESTHETIC EMPATHS AS HEALERS

Empaths who experience synesthesia may have a difficult time working as physical healers, as much of the pain or violence they'll witness will take a serious physical and mental toll on them. However, they are particularly well-suited to bridge the gap between the worlds of medical science and emotional or metaphysical energy, as they are one of the only empath types that are recognized in the scientific realm. They can serve to remind us all of how deeply our actions can impact the people around us, and that pain is a shared experience.

Synesthetic empaths regularly report feeling overwhelmed by human interactions, no matter how mild. As with physical empaths, it is recommended that they offer healing services to one client at a time, in an environment that promotes calm and focus.

ANIMAL EMPATHS

Animal empaths may carry the same empathic abilities and traits as emotional or physical empaths, but with most of their empathy directed towards animals. Many feel more comfortable in the company of animals than humans and are deeply attuned to the animal's needs, fears, desires, and instincts. Their empathic gifts often endear them to animals, even species that are usually deemed too wild or dangerous to form bonds with humans, and animals tend to be drawn to them in turn, feeling calmer in their presence than they do with other people.

Animal empaths are rarer than emotional or physical empaths, and there is a great deal of diversity amongst them in terms of empathic power. Some are able to sense energies emitted from all non-human animals, while some report connections only with a certain species, or with one specific animal. Some animal empaths simply feel a stronger connection to animals than they do with humans, but still manage to maintain perfectly healthy emotional relationships with other people; by contrast, other animal empaths may struggle to relate to humans generally and find interpersonal relationships extremely challenging.

Most animals are deeply empathic themselves. They need to be, as they do not have the ability to communicate with language but must navigate complex group dynamics to stay safe and well-fed. The animal empath often views life through the perspective of an animal, rejecting or rebelling against the trappings of modern society, and preferring to focus on the animal necessities of life: food, shelter from danger, comfort, and unity with nature.

ANIMAL EMPATHS AS HEALERS

Since animal empaths are so sensitive to the energies of animals, they naturally make wonderful veterinarians and caretakers of animals. They can also use their gifts to help humans, though, as animal comfort has proven very effective in treating people with anxiety disorders, depression, and autism, just to name a few conditions. Animals can also be trained to work in service to those with physical or mental disabilities. Animal empaths are uniquely suited to bridge the growing gap between humanity and the animal kingdom, reminding us all to look up to animals instead of looking down on them and to recognize that humans and animals are more similar than we are different.

PLANT EMPATHS

Plant empaths are tapped into the energy of the natural world. They have green thumbs, able to coax plants to grow and thrive, sometimes even under inhospitable conditions, and are more aware than most of the rhythms of nature. Many have no need to consult farmer's almanacs or weather reports to know what's in store for the plants in their garden or farm.

As with animal empaths, the community of plant empaths includes a vast array of different experiences. Some plant empaths get along with other people easily, and simply find that they have a strong penchant for gardening, or feel more comfortable surrounded by a natural landscape; meanwhile, some plant empaths have a very difficult time relating to other humans or animals and tend to use nature as a means of self-isolation. Most plant empaths rely heavily on a physical connection to the natural world in order to feel healthy and happy; in locations where nature is inaccessible, such as deep in the heart of a concrete city, they may quickly become anxious, depressed, or disoriented.

PLANT EMPATHS AS HEALERS

Plant empaths can serve the world as healers in several different fashions. Some plant empaths find their stride in healing other humans and animals through the plant and nutrition-based treatments, working as nutritionists and dieticians, cooks or chefs, homeopathic doctors, crafters of herbal medicine, naturopaths, and so on. Meanwhile, some are better able to apply their healing energies towards plant life exclusively, using their empathic powers to nurture those plants which can best serve the environment, those which can be distilled into medicinal remedies, or those that can best feed their communities.

All plants absorb energy from the sun. Eating an organic, plant-based diet is one of the simplest and most ethically sound ways to consume the energy of life without guilt. Much of the oxygen we breathe is recycled by plants in our environment. The earth's atmosphere and ecosystems rely on thriving plant life to self-sustain. This being the case, many plant empaths are already actively involved in healing efforts without even being aware of it, on a global level. The simple act of nourishing these underserved life forms can have an immeasurable positive impact on society and the environment at large.

GEOMANTIC EMPATHS

Geomantic empaths feel empathetic connections to natural materials or places rather than with living beings. They may also be referred to as "environmental empaths," and they are able to pick up on the energetic vibrations of rocks, trees, mountains, bodies of water, geographic locations, or even distant celestial bodies. Some also feel an affinity with human-built structures and can recognize the energy of past and future events housed within the walls of certain rooms or buildings.

There are two primary forms of geomantic empathy: object-based, and earth-based. Object-based geomantic empaths will feel connections to specific items or buildings, and typically have a strong preference for positively charged items (those with happy histories) or new items that have an energetic blank slate. For these empaths, vintage shopping can be a challenging, unpredictable experience; even new items that are created or sourced unethically may carry a negative charge that impacts them. Museums and historical landmarks may be emotionally overwhelming. Furthermore, finding a place to live can be quite difficult, as most previously inhabited spaces will retain the energies of previous tenants; even if nothing particularly traumatic occurred in the home, it is likely to feel somewhat haunted until space can be energetically cleansed, through smudging or another cleansing ritual.

Earth-based geomantic empaths, by contrast, feel an empathic connection to the elements of the earth in all their various forms. They resonate with organic materials, no matter how large or small: mountains and pebbles, oceans and raindrops, thriving redwood forests and fallen twigs. Some geomantic empaths claim that they are able to communicate with ancient trees which, like Gods, channel energy, and spiritual wisdom through them.

Occasionally, geomantic empaths are able to sense oncoming natural disasters before they occur. This may sound implausible, but when we look at the animal kingdom, we see that this instinctual detection is not at all uncommon or supernatural in nature; rodents, birds, cats, dogs, horses, and elephants will often panic and attempt to flee in the moments before a natural disaster, like an earthquake or tsunami, strikes. These beings may simply be more sensitive than most to the vibrations of the earth, which do shift subtly during cataclysmic events.

GEOMANTIC EMPATHS AS HEALERS

Geomantic empaths can be effective healers in several arenas. They can be especially well-suited to energy healing practices that involve crystal work, such as chakra alignment or geomancy. Geomantic empaths may benefit from the study of the principles of sacred geometry and apply these theories to landscaping or interior design. Empathically informed home and garden design can be an integral aspect of any long-term healing journey.

Rare Empath types

The following categories of empathic power are extremely rare to encounter. This being the case, there are many skeptics who question whether or not these forms of empathic ability actually exist, and judge those who claim to harness them as frauds. Typically, those who are skeptical of these abilities also fail to understand the nuance of these categories, lumping them all together under one umbrella or confusing one type for another. In truth, very few empaths who identify with the below categories claim to possess supernatural abilities, such as telepathy or the ability to move items with the mind. Instead, most simply claim to be able to tap into energetic frequencies that the rest of us are oblivious to.

Furthermore, most will refer to these abilities as "gifts" rather than "powers" because they aren't always able to determine when, where, or how they use them. Often, these empath types receive extra-sensory messages from the universe that are confusing, disjointed, irrelevant to their personal lives, and inconveniently timed. It is very rare for these empaths to find opportunities to use their sensitivities for personal gain, and many have a number of blind spots in their own lives, despite their incredible insight into the lives of others.

INTUITIVE EMPATHS (ALSO CALLED CLAIRCOGNIZANT EMPATHS)

The gifts of the Intuitive empath are frequently exaggerated in media depictions, which is perhaps why so many people confuse them with precognitive and channel empaths. Intuitive empaths don't have any more insight into the future than anyone else would, in their position; it's the present that they are especially sensitive to, as they are able to detect more than just the emotional and physical energies of others around them, but also their specific energetic frequencies. This means that while an intuitive empath may not have insight on absolutely everything, like your name, your age, your profession, or where you were born, they might immediately sense upon meeting you that you have butterflies in your stomach because you're falling in love with someone new, or that you are on edge because you narrowly escaped a car accident on your way to see them. An emotional empath would only pick up on another person's feelings, while an intuitive empath is more likely to understand the cause and effect of those emotions.

All of us, even those with very low levels of empathetic sensitivity, take in a great deal of information through our senses (sight, sound, smell, taste, and touch) only for our brains to then sort through and disregard, or block out, the majority of it. Our brains do this automatically, sorting through all perceived information and processing only that which it has been trained to see as important or relevant, in order to protect us from getting overwhelmed. To demonstrate this, lift your eyes from the page, let them gloss over and lose focus, then close them for a few moments. Then open them again, and take note of how quickly your eyes choose to focus on one or two items in your view. Also, take note of just how many details your eyes naturally overlook—the color of the floor, the color of the walls, cracked paint, a pile of dust in the corner, the smear on the window pane. If you couldn't ignore these insignificant details, chances are you'd never be able to form a coherent thought or string a few words together into a sentence, because you'd be drowning in information overload at all times.

Intuitive empaths have to use the same strategy to protect themselves from overstimulation; only they often have to learn to shut out a much larger percentage of the sensory information available to them. Many develop coping mechanisms that numb themselves too much of their empathic sensitivities: alcoholism or substance abuse, sex addiction, gambling, and overeating are fairly common behaviors for this empath type. Claircognizants also have a tendency to self-isolate, as the information they pick up on in social situations can often be jarring, unpleasant, and burdensome to carry.

However, these empaths are extremely well-suited to the practice of intuitive counseling or coaching, which we'll touch on in greater detail in chapter 7. Furthermore, they should feel encouraged to connect with empathic healers in other categories, as they can often see the bigger picture in any individual's healing journey; for example, when working with an empathic chiropractor, they may be able to help the practitioner to see their client's stress or anxiety as a factor in their discomfort, or note that the root of their pain is actually based on the dysfunction of an internal organ, rather than a skeletal or muscular issue. They also make wonderful matchmakers between healers and patients, able to sense who will work well together, versus those who might struggle to get onto the same page or effectively communicate with one another.

Channel Empaths (also called Mediums)

Empaths who receive messages from deceased spirits and non-human entities are typically called Channels or Mediums. Some are also able to detect energies from other peoples' past lives. Typically, they receive messages from one distinct point beyond the realm of the living and transmit it to one interested party here on earth. Occasionally, this transmission is an all-encompassing experience for the empath, who embodies the spirit's posture, facial expressions, and speech patterns temporarily.

Channel empaths are extremely rare, though there are many who falsely claim to possess these abilities in order for personal gain. A true channel empath would never aim to exploit another person's grief, so they are not likely to solicit clients or push their services upon anyone. The healing that a true channel empath can offer most people is largely emotional, often focused on grief recovery or a return from a crisis in faith.

Precognitive Empaths (also called Psychic Empaths)

A Precognitive empath, commonly called a psychic, is able to pick up on energetic shifts that indicate future events. This type of empath is frequently misunderstood in popular culture, believed to be mostly fraudulent if they are not able to accurately predict every aspect of the future and name all realities of the present. Precognitive empaths do not claim to be omniscient, however; the energies they detect usually provide them with very limited information, most often delivered through cryptic dreams, the unsettling sensation of déjà vu, jarring visions, or symbolic omens. The messages they receive are frequently abstract and difficult to make sense of until elements of the predicted event begin to fall into place.

Precognitive empaths may identify strongly with the myth of Cassandra, who was given the gift of foresight by Apollo, but then cursed by the very same God with the inability to effectively use her knowledge to impact the future. She was cursed so that no one would ever believe her predictions, despite the fact that they were all accurate. Precognitive empaths often struggle with the basics of interpersonal communication and have a hard time making their voices heard. This may be due to the fact that their insight isn't meant to help them to change the future at all, at least not on their own.

Precognitive empaths will often work as fortune-tellers, an arena which allows them to channel their empathic sensitivities while ultimately leaving it up to their clients to decide

if their predictions will influence the future or
not.

Chapter 4

START WITH YOURSELF

E mpaths are naturally disposed to the healing arts, and often feel a compulsive need to help others. But no one, no matter how deeply empathic, can be an effective healer for others if they aren't willing to invest some of that healing power into themselves, first. To become an empowered empath, you'll need to take some steps to examine your own emotional and physical wounds, work on self-healing, and build enough self-love to stay invested in caring for yourself before others for the rest of your life. This is easier said than done, but it is absolutely necessary. No doctor can perform surgery if they refuse to let their own broken fingers heal. The time and energy you spend on self-healing will pay off in the long run, as it will automatically inspire others to trust in your judgment and value your opinions as deeply as you value them yourself.

WHO ARE YOU, REALLY?

Empaths don't only absorb the emotions, energies, or physical sensations of others. We also take on thoughts, preferences, opinions, and value structures. Many of us spend so much time during our developmental years enmeshed with other people that we have a hard time understanding what we truly think, like, or believe in, ourselves, without the context of our community, friends, family, or work environment to tell us what we *should* be thinking.

One of the first, and most important, steps in your healing journey is to rediscover your core identity. Your core identity is the person that you are without any of the decorations that society places upon us all. If you woke up tomorrow without a career, a bank account, a group of friends, a social media following, a home, a car, a grocery list, a schedule, or a set of responsibilities... what would you do with yourself? How would you choose to spend your time? How would you behave?

Most of us display our core identities in early childhood but quickly lose touch with them as we age and begin to worry about things like our future careers, our sexual identities, or our social popularity. So in order to get back in touch with this part of ourselves, we have to work methodically on peeling back some of our layers. Here we have a step by step guide to getting back to your authentic identity as an adult. The steps can certainly be altered and tailored to suit your personal needs—this is by no means the only way to reconnect with your core identity, but simply an outline to use as a jumping-off point. In this process, it's also important to listen to your gut and follow your instincts to see where they may lead. Don't allow someone else's guidelines to take precedent over your instincts—after all, no one can ever know you as well as you know yourself.

1- **Take some time for yourself** - This may prove challenging, but in order to begin this journey, you'll need to find some alone time in a space where you won't be interrupted or distracted. This could be a retreat or solo vacation, but if time or finances are tight, there is plenty of easily accessible alternatives. This alone time doesn't necessarily need to last more than a few hours, and can be done in the privacy of your own home-- through getting some distance from items that remind you of your constructed identity is recommended, if possible. Go for a walk in the park, or a hike; make arrangements to pet-sit for a friend whose home is less familiar; spend an afternoon at a comfortable table in your favorite café; camp in your own back yard for a night; you could even convert a room in your home into a temporary sanctuary space, draping sheets or scarves over furniture and hiding away photos, tchotchkes, and anything that reminds you of your work life or chores. The point is to break your routine and get a little mental space away from the stressors of your usual daily life.

2- **Find some stillness** – Even when we are alone, in a sanctuary space or nature, most of us are accustomed to constant activity when we are awake. We play with our smartphones and computers; we watch television, we eat mindlessly, we fidget; this inability to be quiet and still is a modern symptom of chronic anxiety that exists on a culture-wide scale. It is one of the primary reasons why some people find meditation arduous. These days, we're all receiving constant reminders that we aren't enough on our own—that we need to be earning more, doing more, owning more; that we need to be busier and more productive and better informed so that we might stand a chance at being happier. In order to reconnect with your authentic self, you need to learn how to silence the voice in your head that wants you to believe you're wasting your time if you aren't doing something with it. Thinking and feeling are both important things to do with our time, and when we are always acting, consuming, or creating, we don't give ourselves nearly enough time or space to do either.

3- **Make a list** – This may sound silly, but I'd urge you to take this part of the process seriously. Once you've gotten some distance from your social and professional spheres, and spent some quiet time on your own, start making a list for yourself, with two columns: one for the things in your life that make you happy, and another for the things that make you angry, sad, or stand in the way of your happiness. Try to remain emotionally objective as you write this list, especially for the column of unhappy realities; you don't want to focus on the negative or pour too much energy into self-pity or the blame game. Also, do your best, to be honest with yourself about these lists—it doesn't matter what other people think you *should* be happy or sad about, what matters is how you actually feel. Your friends and family might think that a happy marriage is the most important goal and that you should be over the moon with your committed partner—but if the relationship isn't working for you, their judgments will never be enough to make you truly happy. Avoid thinking in terms of comparison as much as possible; another person's version of happiness may look and feel completely different than your own.

4- **Honest self-reflection** – This is often the hardest part of the process, so it's perfectly fine to take a break before this step and come back to it when you have plenty of energy and enthusiasm to pour into it. First, evaluate your two-column list, and ask yourself some questions. How might you bring the items in your "happy" column into your life on a more consistent basis? How might you shield yourself from the things that make you unhappy? How many of these things are within your control? How many are up to other people? How many are up to nature and divine energies? How many of the things in the "unhappy" column are actually *good* for you (like exercise, or sleep)? How many of the things in the "happy" column are detrimental to your well-being, in the long run? Are some of the items in opposite columns feeding into each other in a cyclical way, perhaps? And how many of the things that make you "unhappy" are things you invited—or still continue to invite—into your life yourself? There are no right or wrong answers here, and plenty of other probing questions to ask. The real point, though, is to try and get a sense of how much power you truly hold over your own happiness. Many people feel as though they are at the mercy of the world—that things happen to them, and their only option is to react. In truth, though, we are all able to make choices that invite happiness in and shield us from unneeded sources of anxiety and negativity. Pain is a part of life, and can't be avoided completely, but there is a great difference between processing inevitable pain, and feeding into your own chronic suffering. While it may be initially painful to reflect on some of this list, it will ultimately serve to highlight some important truths, such as: How much of your energy is spent serving your happiness, and how much is spent on feeding other peoples' satisfaction? How much of your unhappiness is due to the guilt, frustration, resentment, or shame that comes after making poor choices? Remember, this isn't a time for self-flagellation; self-awareness is our primary goal. Everyone makes poor choices sometimes. Try to forgive yourself; it's the first step in moving forward and breaking unhealthy patterns.

5- **Get creative and playful** – After the previous step, you may be feeling a bit raw, vulnerable, emotional, anxious, or frustrated with yourself. If so, you'll want to throw yourself into a drastic change right away. But before you do anything impulsive, try to take some time to remind yourself of your strengths. Creative expression is one of many excellent ways to do this; it helps us to practice resourcefulness, to think outside the box, to take chances, to work on problem-solving in a way that's enjoyable rather than stressful; furthermore, it can help give us more insight into the inner workings of our souls, helping deeply repressed emotions and thoughts to rise to the surface, and reminding us to listen to our own instincts. If you don't identify as a particularly creative person, you can still gain a lot from the practice of free-journaling, for instance, or dabbling in artistic endeavors without the intention of ever showcasing your work. You can also express creativity through cooking, gardening, or woodworking, for example. Whatever you choose, simply keep in mind that your goal is to find something that allows you to be playful—to be creative without worrying about what is right or wrong, without deadlines, without comparing your creation to someone else's. You want to create in the same way that children do, removing self-doubt and anxiety from the equation. This way, the things you create will be authentic projections of your core identity. If you are a painter, for instance, you may note that the paintings you make for yourself feature different color schemes or stylistic elements, as compared to those you create for an audience.

6- **Make an action plan** – This step can be a constantly evolving process; there's no need to rush it or put a strict deadline on any aspect of your personal growth. However, it is important to start making some concrete plans to move forward that will help to invite more authentic joy into your life and break negative cycles. This may mean taking steps to change your career, spending more time on a hobby or recreational activity that you've previously neglected, or working to remove yourself from relationships that take your energy away from your happiness. You might aim to start small, perhaps by incorporating five minutes of meditation into your daily routine, or you might feel ready to do something more extreme, such as picking up and moving to a warmer, sunnier climate. Whatever choice you make, be prepared for some pushback; it usually takes more than one person to keep a routine in place, and the things that are making you unhappy might actually be working really well for the other people in your life. Acknowledge feelings like fear, guilt, or obligation, but try not to let them rule you. It can be immensely helpful to work through those feelings with a therapist or emotional coach.

7- **Rewrite your personal story** – This can be difficult to do with people who've already known you for a long time, but one deeply empowering step in this process is to work on describing yourself differently when introduced to new acquaintances. As an example, an empathic aspiring author who has spent years around people who invalidate their talents might introduce themselves in a self-deprecating way, describing their day job as "just something I do to pay the bills." But when they begin to validate their authentic identity by confidently telling others: "I am a writer," they'll begin to rewire their own thought patterns and change not only the way they look at themselves but also the way they are perceived by others. They'll automatically feel empowered to invest more time and energy into their craft, and project a level of authenticity that will persuade others to take them seriously as a writer. This same theory can apply to all sorts of situations; a person leaving an abusive relationship, for instance, might rewrite their personal story to describe themselves as a "survivor" rather than as a "victim." A stay-at-home dad might choose to describe himself as "a caregiver *and* a mathematician." Finally, this process doesn't need to be centered on career identities or family roles. One beautiful and transformative experience is to proudly declare, for the first time, that you are an empath, first and foremost.

LEARNING TO LISTEN TO YOUR BODY

Our modern society places a great deal of value on intellect, practicality, and rationality. Most of us receive hundreds of implicit messages daily from the media, economic marketplace, and even our communities, reminding us that our thoughts should be honored over our feelings or emotions. Often, we are told that our feelings are invalid if we cannot find a rational way to explain or justify them. For example, a person who is dissatisfied in a romantic relationship may be advised by magazine articles, television shows, and even their family or friends, to remain involved with their partner unless they can cite a rational explanation for their dissatisfaction. They may be repeatedly asked what their partner has done wrong or encouraged to reconsider their feelings if the partner does not "deserve" to be broken up with. What this person may not be asked, however, is whether or not they feel good about who they are within the context of the relationship; whether they feel a spark or a sense of sentimentality for their partner, or if they simply feel bored and anxious around them.

Too frequently, we become so preoccupied with our thoughts that we forget actually to experience our feelings. Our emotional and physical bodies are both very wise and will work hard to protect us from things that drain or damage us. Even if our minds can't find a legitimate reason to object to certain circumstances in our lives, our bodies will consistently work to clue us into the fact that something needs to change.

Mindfulness meditation is one of the easiest ways to get back into the habit of listening to our bodies. Talk therapy can also be immensely helpful if you find yourself struggling in this area. Those of us who grow up in emotionally repressed environments may have a difficult time deciphering the difference between a feeling and a thought, or in naming specific emotions; there is no shame in this, so long as you are willing to seek guidance from others and work to be conscious of your own feelings.

Chapter 5

THE BASICS OF BOUNDARIES

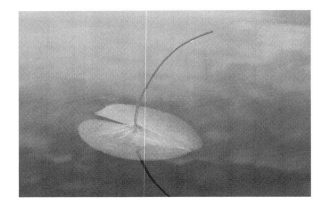

No matter what type of empath you are, regardless of the degree of sensitivity you manage, and whether you harbor aspirations to become a healer or not, it is essential that you develop a healthy sense of personal boundaries. Empaths typically struggle to manage their personal boundaries throughout their lives—even those who are especially empowered and emotionally balanced can find it difficult to maintain their boundaries under pressure, during stressful periods, or at times when they feel a sense of obligation. This being the case, you should never feel ashamed of the fact that strong boundaries do not come naturally to you, and be ready to forgive yourself for making occasional missteps as you work to improve in this area.

WHAT ARE THE BOUNDARIES?

Boundaries are, in essence, honored personal limits. They can apply to physical, emotional, or mental space; they can apply to interpersonal relationships of all kinds; they can apply to matters of health, privacy, financial well-being, energy, productivity, and more. Boundaries help us to manage the manner in which we are treated by others and by ourselves. A person without strong boundaries is a walking target for energy vampires, narcissistic abusers, frauds and dangerous institutions (such as multi-level marketing schemes, spiritual cults, or hate-based organizations); to these emotional predators, an empath without strong boundaries appears to be practically begging to be taken advantage of, used, exploited, scapegoated, and eventually enmeshed or discarded. By contrast, an empath who understands their own boundaries and knows how to enforce them when necessary emits energy that emotional predators will not be attracted to in quite the same way—energy that says firmly, though not aggressively, "I am **not** somebody that you want to mess with."

When a person knows their own boundaries, they know approximately how much they can handle, in all areas of life, and they are comfortable being honest with themselves or others about their own limitations. Knowing where their boundaries lie, they are able to say no to requests and invitations that would be too draining for them to accept and do not allow themselves to feel haunted by a sense of guilt or emotional debt after their refusal. They work consistently on managing expectations, whether these are the expectations that others put upon them, or the expectations they have of other people, to combat unnecessary stress and anxiety. They avoid taking on more than they can handle and purposefully set themselves up for future success by prioritizing self-care. They do not allow other people to dictate the terms of their lives for them. They take responsibility for their own happiness, health, and well-being above all else.

But boundaries aren't just about shutting out things that you know you cannot manage. A person with healthy boundaries uses them to thrive, not just survive. They know what circumstances help them to function at their highest energetic frequency, and use boundaries to invite those circumstances into their lives while distancing themselves from probable distractions, sources of negativity or self-doubt, and anything else that poses a threat to their progress and well-being.

If you picture your body, mind, and soul as a house, then your boundaries are not only the fences that you build around the property to keep dangers and threats out; your boundaries are also the pathways that you build leading to and from the house, guiding you to the places where you most want or need, to be. Boundaries are used for the sake of protection and self-preservation, but also for inspiration, motivation, productivity, and joy.

It's important to note that boundaries can exist in many degrees of intensity. Some people have extremely rigid boundaries, and tolerate very little that is not on their established agenda; meanwhile, others (many empaths, especially) have overly porous or weak boundaries, allowing the needs of others to supersede their own under very light pressure or mild persuasion. Some empaths who are new to boundary work may need to create fairly rigid boundaries initially, in order to put an end to negative cycles in toxic relationships.

Eventually, though, the goal is to maintain healthy boundaries that are fluid, or flexible, with a sturdy foundation. Life is unpredictable, and all energies (including people, places, things, and feelings) are in constant flux. Rigid boundaries can be necessary for the protection in times of distress, but they can also be severely limiting in the long-term. A person with flexible boundaries can allow themselves to apply different standards to all the different types of relationships in their life; they can maintain certain standards during times of peace, but shift their limits to accommodate unexpected changes, like a family emergency or an unbelievable career opportunity; and most importantly, they can forgive others for transgressing over their boundaries, forgive themselves for allowing such transgressions, and continue moving forward, chasing happiness and fulfillment.

How do I know if my boundaries are reasonable?

This answer may be initially frustrating to read, but it is the honest truth. No one can define what boundaries are reasonable for other people. The only person who can fairly judge whether or not your boundaries are plausible, fair, valid, or sustainable, is you.

This means there will be some trial and error as you work to establish boundaries that serve you. Sometimes, you may find that your boundaries are easily accepted by others, but maintaining or enforcing them causes you more stress than they are worth. At other points, you may find that your established boundaries, which initially seemed reasonable and necessary to you, are rejected, invalidated, or ignored by most, or all, other people. In some cases, your preferred boundaries may prove to be entirely impossible to maintain while respecting the laws of physics, nature, or the country in which you live.

Personally, I would love to maintain a boundary that prevents me from having to pay taxes on my income, but I can't really implement this boundary without taking some of my other boundaries down in the process—specifically, the boundary of needing to live free, outside of prison.

There are some who will pressure you to adjust, or even dismantle, your preferred boundaries, using guilt, obligation, and unreasonable comparisons to convince you that your boundaries are not healthy. Empaths are often predisposed to putting the needs of others before their own and tend to feel quite selfish and self-indulgent when we begin to focus on serious self-care rituals, so it's important that we guard ourselves against these types of detractors. Ask yourself: what might this person (or group of people, or organization) stand to gain by convincing me to adjust my boundaries here? And furthermore, ask yourself: If taken to the extreme, what might I stand to lose by allowing them to persuade me beyond my own limits successfully?

In some cases, these evaluating questions might help you to see that the person in question truly has your best interest at heart as they attempt to negotiate your boundaries; for example, a friend might try to convince a shy, reserved, or overly cautious empath to take a step outside of their comfort zone, and try karaoke, or roller-coaster riding, to encourage them to take some risks and have fun. In this instance, it would be up to the empath to decide for themselves if they should accept the invitation to alter their boundaries. However, these questions will sometimes lead you to see that your boundaries are in fact reasonable and necessary for self-preservation and that by weakening them, the person (or people) in question only stands to gain at your expense.

HOW CAN I ESTABLISH MY BOUNDARIES?

When you feel confident in the boundaries you've defined for yourself, you might want to shout them from the rooftops—or at least explain them to some of the people who are nearest and dearest to you. However, in many cases—especially for those who are new to boundary work—early conversations about boundaries tend to backfire. Verbally establishing boundaries with someone whom you are not actively engaged in a conflict with can feel, for the receiving party, very confrontational, accusatory, and condescending, no matter how kindly the message is delivered.

It may feel anticlimactic to define your boundaries without explicitly communicating them to other people—a bit like writing a book and never publishing it—but in truth, most boundaries do not need to be stated or formally established right away. Even if your boundaries are not being respected, there are practical ways to enforce them without sitting your friend, lover, parent, or colleague down and saying: "These are my boundaries, and henceforth, you must observe and respect them if you wish to avoid punitive consequences."

Of course, in some circumstances, it may eventually become necessary to have such a conversation, but generally, stating boundaries in this way can actually work to stir up conflict rather than solve a problem. Instead, it may be most helpful to think of your boundaries as a contract that you keep with yourself. Ultimately, you have no control over how others behave or how they treat you, whether you communicate your boundaries or not; but you always have control over your own actions, reactions, thoughts, and behaviors.

As a working example, let's look at a theoretical empath—we'll call her Nadia—who has a very close relationship with her boss, Lisa. Lisa is an entrepreneur who built her own business from the ground up and has been burning the candle at both ends since she opened her business several years ago. She hired Nadia as a personal assistant when her business was still very small; the two of them bonded and became good friends as the size of Lisa's company grew. Lisa trusts Nadia above all her other employees and prefers to work with her exclusively whenever possible. She finds that Nadia is the best person to turn to for help in a pinch and that Nadia has a special ability to anticipate her needs and prevent most problems before they even have a chance to arise. She regularly tells Nadia things like: "I don't know what I would do without you," or "I need you here—don't you ever leave me!" Lisa thinks that she has a great relationship with Nadia because Nadia is always there for her when she needs her. Because she relies so heavily on Nadia's help, she has decided that now is a good time to start a family, knowing that she can put more of her personal responsibilities in Nadia's hands when things get hectic.

Meanwhile, Nadia is feeling totally drained by their professional and personal relationship and really wants things to change. She does not want to quit her job, as the pay is good, and she believes the work experience in this field will be great for her resume and help her to build her own career. She has attempted to gently enforce some boundaries in the past, saying no to picking up extra unpaid hours and insisting that her vacation requests be honored and respected. However, when Lisa tells Nadia that she is pregnant and plans to lean even more heavily on Nadia for help moving forward, Nadia recognizes that it's time to get serious about defining and enforcing her boundaries at work, or she will have to quit.

Since Lisa is her boss, with control over Nadia's livelihood and career reputation, Nadia does not feel comfortable confronting her. Furthermore, since Lisa is pregnant and her moods are impacted by hormonal flux, Nadia wants to take special care to avoid "poking the bear," so to speak; she worries that having a direct and honest conversation about boundaries might backfire and inspire Lisa to become upset with her, which is a completely reasonable fear. Nadia realizes that she can do very little to predict or control Lisa's behavior in the coming months, so instead, she decides to strengthen her boundaries from the inside out—to focus on how her own behavior can work to protect her from energy depletion, emotional burnout, and other effects of personal devaluation. Nadia makes a boundary contract with herself, one that she believes she can always honor, no matter what happens or who she is interacting with. She decides that she will not take on any responsibilities that lie outside of her initial job description—no babysitting, no housework, no running errands for Lisa, no work before 9 am or after 5 pm, and absolutely no unpaid work. If other staff members quit, she will not pick up their slack, but instead, encourage Lisa to hire a replacement as soon as possible. If Lisa attempts to contact her outside of working hours for anything other than an emergency, Nadia will not answer her phone or reply to emails. Furthermore, Nadia decides that she will tolerate only one major emotional outburst from Lisa during the pregnancy or in the year following the birth, after which point, she will have to remind her boss that lashing out is unacceptable and that she will not put up with it a second time. If Lisa attempts to transgress over any of these boundaries more than once, Nadia will start looking for a different job.

Can you see how this set of boundaries is more reliant on Nadia's choices than on Lisa's behavior? Can you also see how it works in Nadia's favor to wait to confront Lisa until a boundary is crossed, rather than pre-emptively warning her not to have an emotional outburst? Realistically, Nadia could use these boundaries to effect major changes in her work environment without ever having to declare them out loud. Her behavior will help to communicate her limits more effectively than her words ever could. Finally, her choice to leave the job if her boundaries aren't respected will help to prevent her from falling into a toxic cycle of abuse.

What do I do if others fail to respect my established boundaries?

Some people struggle to respect boundaries in general; others may simply struggle to respect specific boundaries that are important to you. Whatever the case, it is helpful to recognize that anyone who is repeatedly transgressing over your boundaries is only able to do so because you are allowing them to. If requests, conversations, or arguments fail to get the point across or effect change, you do not need to get tangled up in a cyclical conflict; instead, you can remove yourself from the equation entirely, and stop giving the offending party any opportunity to disrespect your boundaries.

As a general rule, it's good to keep in mind that those who become angry or irritable about your boundaries are exactly the same people you should be using boundaries to protect yourself from. Anyone who respects you as a unique and equally valuable individual would work to understand and respect your boundaries, even if they found them initially confusing; they would ask you to clarify or help them to better see where your limits are. By contrast, someone who is angered by your establishment of personal limitations most likely does not see you as an equal; they see you as a source of some form of energy that they can use and exploit, whether they are conscious of it or not. If this is the case, it's very unlikely that you'll be able to convince them that your boundaries are worthy of respect. You may find it much more effective to simply reduce your exposure to this person, or cut off contact entirely.

Sometimes, this may not be an option, as with a family member who relies on you, or with someone that you rely upon. In these cases, it's generally helpful to focus on asking for the behavior that you *do* want to see from them, rather than chastising them for the unwanted behavior. For instance, if your parent frequently shows up at your home without warning, and you want this to stop, you may find it more effective to say: "I wish you would let me know when you're planning to come by, so that I could make sure I have free time to enjoy your company," as opposed to saying: "You can't come here unannounced anymore, it's driving me crazy!"

What if I don't understand, or cannot respect someone else's boundary?

If you didn't develop healthy boundaries by the time you reached adulthood, then chances are you grew up around some authority figures who didn't model them for you. This means that, even while you may now understand the need to have your own boundaries, you still may encounter some people whose boundaries seem totally unreasonable to you.

Even if another person's boundary seems illogical, ridiculous, vengeful, arbitrary, or otherwise objectionable, it's important to try and respect it. You don't have to like it; you might ask the person in question to further clarify their stance, to help you understand, but they do not owe you such an explanation, so they may not be willing to do this. Even so, you should do your absolute best to respect the boundary if you expect anyone else to respect yours.

Chapter 6

WALKING BEFORE YOU RUN

M any empaths find that establishing, enforcing, and protecting their personal boundaries is a lifechanging step. After spending a lifetime allowing others to casually trespass over your limits without consequence, fortifying your boundaries will help you to feel empowered and replenished, as you will be able to channel more of your energy into activities and emotions that serve you rather than drain you, avoid sources of negativity, and prevent some conflicts before they even have a chance to arise.

Still, it's important to be cautious moving forward, and recognize that reaching the peak of a mountain in personal development does not mean that all the hard work is over, nor does it mean that you are now impervious to setbacks or emotional contagion. Often, empaths get a rush of empowerment during the first few weeks or months after they begin to focus on defining and maintaining their boundaries pointedly, only to then grow lazy about their boundary maintenance, slowly but surely sliding back into their old habits; or, alternatively, they may become discouraged when their newly strengthened boundaries are continually challenged by difficult people or powerful institutions. It can be heartbreaking for the newly awakened or empowered empath to learn that boundaries, while extremely powerful, cannot protect them from everyone and everything. Learning this through experience can sometimes trigger a temporary loss of faith in the empowerment process, or a spell of depression, anxiety, reclusiveness, or toxic anger.

For this reason, it is recommended that all empaths allow themselves adequate time to heal personally and enjoy their fulfillment before diving into any training program or beginning to heal others regularly. To be an effective empath healer, perspective and experience will be two of your most valuable tools. Even the most enlightened and empowered among us can fall, but the seasoned empathic healer recognizes that the pain of a fall can be channeled and used as fuel to refocus on personal evolution and elevation. In truth, there are no missteps and no setbacks—there are only lessons. It is up to you whether you choose to reject those lessons or embrace them as gifts from the universe.

THE WOUNDED HEALER

Many empath healers actually utilize their own painful experiences to inspire others, connect with clients on a deeper level, and improve the quality of their healing work. They do not shy away from their past wounds; they do not deny or attempt to hide them. Instead, they see them as one of their greatest points of strength, and recognize their transformative power, crediting painful past experiences for their current perspective and insight. They embrace their past wounds as a part of their journey and an integral aspect of their identity, sustaining the radical notion that one does not need to be perfect in order to teach others or to be a leader. Frequently, these empaths find that the work of healing others helps them to cure their own internal pain, as well.

Yet the wounded healer does need to be reminded, at times, that there is no substitute for true self-care. Even if the act of healing others is rewarding, cathartic, soothing, and productive, it can easily be overdone to the point of personal detriment. Recognize that projection and self-avoidance are risk factors for you; schedule physical, mental, emotional, and energetic check-ups for yourself on a regular basis, and be mindful not to take on too many clients who remind you of your younger self, or whose situations bring up triggering memories for you. Wounded healers have a tendency to dwell in pain that reminds them of their own, rather than addressing their wounds and working to heal them. Always remember: the healthier you are, the better-quality care you can provide for your clients.

STAYING OPEN-MINDED

Even amongst the most empathic people, certain beliefs, values, and healing styles carry a stigma that often inspires the reactions of skepticism, negativity, and closed-mindedness.

No matter where you fall on the empathy scale, chances are that your personal opinions and perspective are polluted, at least in part, by the value judgments of those around you: people you love, people you respect, and sometimes, people you fear. Perhaps you've grown up in a household that respected the power of non-western medicines and homeopathy but mocked or derided concepts like astrology or geomancy. Alternatively, maybe you currently find yourself surrounded by a community of people who embrace energy healing and naturopathy, but firmly reject any ideas, sentiments, or rituals that are too reminiscent of formalized religion or spiritual faith.

Therefore, it may be necessary to forcefully remind yourself to keep an open mind and open heart as you experiment with healing methods and schools of thought that are unfamiliar to you.

At the end of the day, there is very little to be gained from tearing down another person's faith, however misguided they might appear to be. If you encounter tools or ideas in your empathic healing journey that strike you as truly dangerous, remember that it is always possible to affect change and prevent harm without invalidating another person's belief system.

As an example, let's look at the concept of climate change. Say you are a firm believer that climate change is a human-made problem, and that extreme measures should be taken by all people on earth to reduce needless waste and pollution, immediately and with enthusiasm, in order to prevent future natural disasters. You encounter a soul who believes wholeheartedly that climate change is a lie—a scare tactic devised by scientists and the media, designed to frighten us all into embracing policy changes that will make money for large corporations at the expense of the general populace—and that most scientific claims, like evolution, are a load of hogwash because they contradict with the histories and explanations spelled out plainly in the Christian Bible. This person's refusal to consider scientific evidence might frustrate you to no end; you might even feel that it is unsafe to allow their school of thought to thrive, and feel a strong urge to correct their beliefs.

But what will you really accomplish by showing this person scientific "proof" that their belief system is invalid? Most often, humans hold onto beliefs that are comforting to them. When you try to strip down or invalidate ideas that make people happy, they are more likely to end up despising you than they are to change their minds.

You can still work towards your goal of preventing harm without tearing down this person's source of comfort. Even if they don't believe that climate change is a result of human behavior, they may be convinced to reduce their carbon footprint through other motivations; improved air quality can positively impact the health of their children, for example; or, conversion from coal to wind energy might be painted as an amazing economic opportunity for their family and community at large. This is an example of constructive problem-solving. There is no need to negate the ideas that others value— you can accept another person's truth, and add your perspective to it, rather than viewing your two contrasting belief systems as foes in a fight to the death. Belief is never a zero-sum game. By opening your mind up to acceptance and constructive communication, you may actually be surprised by the wisdom of those you "disagree" with.

In conflict resolution, or whenever you encounter ideas or beliefs that you feel the urge to fight against, keep these concepts in mind to stay constructive:

- Expansion, rather than limitation
- Enhancement, rather than a detraction
- Addition, rather than subtraction
- Creation, rather than destruction
- Acceptance, rather than skepticism
- Inclusion, rather than exclusion

- Receptiveness in place of defensiveness
- Hope and faith, in place of fear and doubt

Refrain from judgment and do your best to suspend your disbelief. Stay open to the limitless possibilities of the universe. Belief is a powerful energetic tool.

HONORING YOUR WORTH

Generally, empaths can struggle to advocate for themselves and ask for reciprocity in any type of relationship, whether it is personal or professional. Particularly when empaths begin healing work, many of us have a difficult time monetizing our efforts. When we become caregivers to those in need, we tend to over-empathize with our patients' pain, and feel awkward, or afraid to ask for financial compensation. Most of us are accustomed to giving and giving and giving without getting much in return, but if you are truly driven to become a healer, you must learn to nip this habit in the bud, establish firm boundaries surrounding reciprocity, and embrace your own worth.

Time, attention, and compassion are all highly valuable entities. A common misstep that empath healers make is undervaluing their own offerings. For example, an empath who still carries the weight of the persecution wound may feel that they cannot charge as much money for an energy healing session of ninety minutes as a licensed psychiatrist would charge for a session of the same length.

When you undervalue your own work, you sell yourself short, and you stifle your own healing energy by making your work unsustainable. No one can work tirelessly in any field that fails to provide them with enough financial stability to thrive. Underselling your worth will eventually lead to burnout and compassion fatigue, which may, in turn, compromise your reputation and destroy the sense of fulfillment you would otherwise glean from healing work.

Look to other empathic healers that you admire for cues here. How do they market themselves? What are their pricing structures like? How are their client reviews? If they're someone you look up to; chances are they've managed to find a formula that works for their clients *and* themselves.

There's nothing wrong with using a little trial and error to find your sweet spot for financial compensation. Always remember that your pricing structure will send a subconscious message to your prospective clients about how much you value your own time and energy. If you underprice your services, it may not be long before you find yourself surrounded by energy vampires who feel entitled to your time and attention, despite having nothing to give in return.

OFFERING GUIDANCE, NOT CONTROL

Empath healers can often find themselves filling leadership roles in the lives of others, whether they intend to or not. When an empath becomes empowered, they emit an energetic glow that naturally attracts those who are in need of guidance and healing themselves; these people tend to thrust empowered empaths into roles like that of a guru, life coach, spiritual guide, or teacher.

When this happens, it can be challenging on multiple fronts. Many empaths aren't used to being the center of attention, being looked up to, being given space to speak without interruption or negation, or being seen as an authority figure. This form of power can be unfamiliar to empaths, and thus, some fail to mature into these roles gracefully. They may become overwhelmed by their new sense of responsibility for the well-being of others; or, alternatively, they may allow this power to go to their heads, in which case they may start to see their followers less as students or patients, and more like avatars in a video game, an extension of the empath's identity that they can, and should, control.

This becomes even more challenging when the empath's followers are engaged in risky behaviors or toxic relationships, and are not able, for whatever reason, to alter the dangerous circumstances of their lives urgently. If you are considering taking the plunge and offering your services as a healer, therapist, or counselor of any kind, take a moment right now to pause and evaluate your own ability to resist the temptation to control. Most of us like to believe that we would never want to control other people—that such a desire goes against our very nature—but realistically, when the going gets rough, the impulse to exert control over those who rely on us for guidance can switch on very suddenly, like a light switch. Just ask any parent of a running toddler—when someone you care for is endangering themselves, instinct takes over, and it generally chooses to use force rather than gentle guidance. If a toddler were running towards a busy intersection, most of us would, understandably, choose to scoop them up in our arms and take them elsewhere, rather than gently urging them to stay mindful of their surroundings.

Imagine your closest and dearest friend has come to you looking for support, and confesses that they have been managing an addiction to heroin in secret for the past year, unbeknownst to anyone else in their life; or, if it fits this friend's character better, imagine them admitting that their romantic partner has been physically abusive to them for the past three months.

Ask yourself first: Would you be able to keep this information to yourself, and share it only with your own therapist or counselor, or with a legal authority when and if you believed someone's life to be in danger?

Ask yourself second: would you be able to continue providing support, guidance, and compassion if this friend took no steps at all to change their circumstances and protect themselves?

If the answer to either of these questions is a "no," then you may not be ready to begin healing work for others. You can get there, but first, you will need to take some time to focus on acceptance and review your boundary work.

The desire to interfere when others invite toxicity into their own lives is not something to be ashamed of. It can be extremely frustrating for the empathic healer to find that someone who values their judgments and asks for their advice doesn't always want to follow the path that the empath recommends for them. Not only can it feel exhausting, like continually pouring water into a bottomless well—it can also feel frightening and dangerous for the empath, who shares in the pain and suffering that others expose themselves to. If you are emotionally handcuffed to another person, it's perfectly understandable to want to restrain them from jumping off a cliff's edge physically. As hard as it may be to accept this, though, the right move for the empath healer to take in this scenario is to untether themselves and allow the other party to make unhealthy choices if they want to, rather than holding them back. You cannot save someone who does not want to save themselves, nor can you heal someone who isn't ready to be healthy; the harder you try, the more likely you are to exhaust yourself and erode any trust or respect the person in question holds for you.

It's important to recognize that the role of an empath healer is to enlighten others and offer compassion. It can indeed be tempting to insert oneself into the lives of others in the name of protecting them from themselves, or doing what's best for them, but this practice is not advisable, and usually backfires in one of two ways; either the patient (or student) will suddenly turn around and reject the empath healer, rebelling against their attempts to control their healing journey; or alternatively, they may accept the empath's interference in their lives and grow to rely on it, becoming crippled by their dependence, never learning to make their own choices.

Think of the methods by which parents help their children learn to walk. Most use one or more of the following tactics to accomplish this goal:

1) Modeling the desired behavior (showing the child how to "walk the walk," repeatedly or in an exaggerated manner)

2) Providing incentive and motivation for the desired behavior ("You can eat the cookie on the table if you walk to the table's edge!")

3) Offering support for the desired behavior (either holding the child's hands as they walk forward, or staying nearby with open arms ready to catch them if they should fall)

4) Praising the desired behavior (cheering for the child if they are able to make any progress at all towards the goal of walking on their own two feet, even if the progress is minimal)

It is quite rare for parents to succeed in teaching their children to walk on their own by employing the following tactics:

1) Physically forcing the desired behavior (moving the child's feet into the right position with hands around their ankles)
2) Reprimanding the child's failure to display the desired behavior (yelling at the child for continuing to crawl, or for falling down when they try to walk)
3) Producing the desired behavior on their behalf (placing the child's feet atop the parent's feet as they walk, and expecting the child to then continue the motion on their own)

4) Using threats or intimidation to inspire the desired behavior ("Stand up and walk on your own two feet now, or no dinner for you tonight!")

Learning to make healthy choices for ourselves is perhaps the most vital step in any individual's healing journey. When your guidance and influence crosses the line into forceful, coercive or controlling behavior, you rob your patient or student of the opportunity to learn from their own mistakes, encourage codependency, and undermine their goal of self-determination. You cannot walk the path of healing *for* anyone else—all you can do is show them the map, prepare them for the realities of the voyage, and give them space to find their own way.

- Chapter 7 -

EMOTIONAL HEALING

METHODS

N ow that you have done the work to heal yourself and practice some thorough self-reflection, it may be time to start exploring the different types of healing to which empaths are best suited. This chapter will review healing methods that are likely to work best for emotional empaths, but there is no reason why other empath types should not experiment with these methods if they feel drawn to them.

MEDITATION

Of all the empathic healing methods available, meditation is perhaps the most easily accessible for those with limitations, be they financial, logistical, temporal, or otherwise. Anyone can learn to meditate, at any age, in any place, at any time, for as short or long of a session as they can manage.

Meditation requires at least a few minutes of quiet and stillness. It can be practiced standing, sitting, lying down, or in a challenging yoga pose. The goal is to close your eyes, breathe mindfully, and allow yourself to recognize your own thought patterns without being consumed or overpowered by them. It is a common misconception that you can only successfully meditate with a clear mind. It's not about *not* thinking; it's thinking *about* your thoughts, recognizing that they are only thoughts (not reality) and that you have the power to embrace them or to let them go. Some people prefer to use meditation guides—classes or audio recordings that provide ideas or concepts to meditate upon. Others find it more productive to simply let their mind wander and ride the wave of thoughts, while still staying healthily detached from them. This would allow you to encounter a thought that causes you anxiety— say, for instance, that in the midst of a meditation session, you suddenly remember an overdue bill that you've forgotten to pay—but rather than spinning into a panic or buying into negative beliefs about yourself, your detached mind might instead think: "I wonder why this thought came up at this particular moment. Normally, I'd fly into a panic over this. What other reactions could I choose that might serve me better?"

Though meditation can be simplified into a mental exercise so simple, even kindergartners can grasp it, there is also no end to the potential depth and complexity of this healing art. Incorporating just a few minutes of meditation into your routine on a weekly or daily basis can work to enhance mental and emotional clarity, to replenish energy and focus, and to manage stress. By contrast, doing intense meditative work, whether guided or alone, for extended periods of time—an hour each day, or even multiple hours—can have an extraordinary transformative impact on every aspect of your life, from your physical health to your mental acuity and productivity levels.

Even if you only have time to practice for five minutes a day, meditation is one of the most effective ways to put yourself back in the mental and emotional driver's seat of your own life. When we are overwhelmed by fast-paced schedules, technological acceleration, busy social and familial networks, and constant financial pressures, it can be easy to feel like our lives are happening to us, whether we like it or not. By taking a few minutes to pause and re-center ourselves, we are better able to refocus our energies on the things that matter most; to extract the negative thoughts and feelings that are not ours to carry and are not serving us, and to remember that our lives are mostly what we make of them.

Meditation practices can be extremely productive, sometimes leading to epiphanies, mental breakthroughs, and emotional fulfillment. It isn't always a triumphant experience, though, which is why empaths should feel encouraged to stick to a routine practice for at least a full month before they make any judgments about its value or effectiveness. Sometimes, meditation can lead us through complex emotional experiences, like anger release or trauma resurfacing, both of which can initially lead us to feel temporarily worse before we start to feel better. In the long run, though, meditation is like exercise for the brain and the soul; it strengthens us from the inside out.

CEREMONIAL HEALING

There are many different kinds of ceremonial healing rituals; some are attached to spiritual faiths and derived from ancient traditions, such as Native American, Wiccan or Pagan healing ceremonies, while other New Age traditions aim to incorporate knowledge from multiple cultures and schools of thought, making rituals accessible to experienced practitioners and novices alike.

Ceremonial healing rituals can also be focused on physical ailments, but here, we'll touch on two of the most popular emotional healing methods. You may find many other ritual services are available to you if you contact lightworkers and healers in your area.

ENERGY SHIELDS

Creating an energy shield is something you can do for yourself, even with very little experience. It is largely a mental visualization exercise, in which you imagine a shield of energy drawn around yourself, and define very clearly what you want to let inside, what must be kept out, and what type of energy the shield is made of. Energy shields can be protective or deflective; they can be solid and rigid or woven like a grid to allow certain elements in while guarding against others. They may be drawn to help us accomplish our goals, or they may be created to help us ward off toxic, destructive energies.

If you are struggling to make your own energy shield effective, it may be wise to seek out an energy healer to help with a ceremonial shield creation. This may involve a consultation, meditation, crystal healing work, a sonic healing element, and maybe the repetition of mantras or affirmations. Logistics will vary, depending on the healer you choose to work with. Whatever the process, an energy shield created by two empaths will be exponentially stronger and more tangible than any shield created by a lone individual.

In a ceremony like this, it's important to be as honest and transparent as possible with your healer and to stay open-minded. Their rituals may seem odd to you, but at the end of the day, your energy shield will only ever be as strong as your belief in it.

CORD CUTTING CEREMONY

Often, when we deal with the process of ending toxic relationships, be they romantic, platonic, professional or familial, we assume that proximity or physical exposure to the other party is the primary source of our problem. We behave as though naming the end of the relationship should be enough to foster healing and jumpstart the process of moving on, or as though putting physical distance between ourselves and the other party should be enough to get them out of our heads and hearts.

In reality, relationships are far more complex than we give them credit for, and healing from a toxic relationship can be just as intense as healing from a major physical injury or illness. Relationships aren't just about spending time together; they are about a constant exchange of energy. Even after a relationship is "ended," it is still entirely possible for one or both parties to continue pouring energy into it. Initially, this is unavoidable—any relationship that is deeply important to you will need to be adequately mourned before you'll be able to move on from it. But at a certain point, continuing to dwell on the ending of a toxic relationship, or continuing to hold on to the habits, values, and ideas that were central to it, can be detrimental to your emotional health and well-being. In these instances, a Cord Cutting Ceremony can be just the right thing to help a person move on from a relationship, not simply in a physical sense, but on an energetic, emotional, and metaphysical level.

A Cord Cutting ceremony is meant to address the way that many of us continue to carry the energetic baggage of relationships for weeks, months, or even years after we put an "end" to them, and works to release that unhealthy energy. A successful Cord Cutting can help a person to stop obsessing over what went wrong in the relationship; to end their mind's preoccupation with the other party (many people continue to have recurring dreams about those they've broken up with, or alternatively, their minds play tricks on them and convince them that they see or hear this person all over the place, even when they aren't actually present); to stop attracting similar people into their lives or creating similarly toxic relationships with others; and to release themselves from value judgements that belong to the past relationship rather than to their present identity and circumstances.

One easy example of why a Cord Cutting Ceremony can be necessary is the concept of "rebounding." Popular culture reinforces the idea that we are only complete when we are involved with someone else, so many of us have internalized the idea that the best way to get over someone is to "get right back up on the horse" and replace them with another person. While there's certainly nothing wrong with choosing to date casually after the ending of a toxic relationship, the fact is that it isn't always necessary or healthy to jump back into the dating pool if a person still has personal healing work to do. If you end a relationship and still feel haunted afterward by a sense of pressure to become emotionally involved with someone new (or multiple new people), this may be a sign that you are still being fueled by the energy of the previous relationship, more so than you are driven by your own authentic desires and needs. Feeling a sense of competition with an ex-lover or friend, or fantasizing about revenge, are both ways that you can continue to participate in a relationship, even after it is "over."

A Cord Cutting ceremony will release you from another person's emotional grip, allowing your energy to rise up, finally untethered, and truly free.

TALK THERAPY

There are a few different schools of established and respected thought within the world of talk therapy, but generally speaking, it is a process in which an individual (or group of individuals in a relationship or family unit) can work on self-reflection and self-improvement with the assistance of an objective third party.

Empaths can be particularly well-suited to the therapy profession because we are often able to put people at ease, communicate even with the most guarded individuals, and read subtle, non-verbal cues that can provide enormous insight into the internal workings of others' minds. Patients in talk therapy are generally hoping to receive some compassionate understanding from the professional sitting opposite them, along with constructive recommendations for growth and change. Unfortunately, there are plenty of people who have chosen to become therapists who lack the ability to make their clients emotionally comfortable or to be sensitive to their clients' sore spots and triggers. Empaths can be a much-needed counterbalance to these types, creating safe spaces that are emotionally welcoming, nurturing, and validating.

The empathic therapist may struggle, though, with restraint. An important part of therapy work is self-reflection, self-revelation, and the development of self-awareness; none of these things can be accomplished when a therapist does too much of the work, or emotional processing, on their patient's behalf. If someone is simply told: "The root of all your relationship problems is your fractured relationship with your own mother," the chances are that they will react with skepticism or even hostility, as it makes most people very uncomfortable to be seen by others in a way that they cannot see themselves. However, if they are able to come to this realization on their own terms, they will be better able to incorporate this idea into their healing journey, and better motivated to work on personal growth, feeling empowered rather than vulnerable and ashamed. This can be difficult for empaths, which can often read people very quickly and detect the root of their frustrations ages before the person in question develops enough self-awareness to catch wise.

Furthermore, empaths who choose to work as therapists must take great care to avoid emotional contagion and burnout by focusing on self-care and maintaining firm boundaries with their clients. Therapists often work with people who are suffering from an immense amount of emotional pain, some of whom may have repressed their empathetic impulses, which can make them difficult to work with, and even cruel at times. Working with malignant narcissists, for example, or violent psychopaths, is certainly an admirable choice and a valuable way to contribute your empathic gifts to a worthy cause, but it can also be extremely draining and emotionally damaging to work with these kinds of people. Empath therapists must be vigilant and ready to recognize the symptoms of compassion fatigue and emotional burnout in themselves; otherwise, if they push themselves too hard, they run the risk of numbing themselves to their own feelings or becoming cynical and losing faith in the effectiveness of their own healing efforts.

Some people seek out therapy when they have a genuine desire to break the negative cycles in their lives. Others may seek out therapy without harboring any earnest desire to learn from their mistakes, grow, or change; instead, they may simply wish for attention, coddling, and pity.

Learning to recognize the difference between clients who want your help, and clients who want to use you for self-gratification will save you a great deal of frustration in the long run.

INTUITIVE COUNSELING

Intuitive counseling is very similar to talk therapy but incorporates the therapist's empathic sensitivities to a far greater extent. An intuitive counselor will look beyond the framework of traditional psychotherapy and use their empathic instincts to help patients to uncover repressed or buried truths about themselves. Intuitive counselors may also make more specific recommendations to their patients, providing actionable advice where most traditional therapists would only be able to generalize.

Intuitive counselors should still aim to respect the same patient-therapist boundaries that a therapist would. The primary difference lies in the fact that they are honest with their clients about their ability to pick up on unspoken cues, and that they may use intuitive information to inform their work in sessions. As an example, an intuitive counselor might handle work with a client in an abusive marriage very differently than a traditional therapist would; the traditional therapist would not be at liberty to push their client to examine the realities of their marriage unless the client expressed concerns themselves. The intuitive counselor, by contrast, would be able to say: "I've picked up on some negative energies surrounding your marriage, and I wonder if we can begin addressing that in our session today. Am I reading this energy accurately?"

Many intuitive counselors also hold degrees in social work or psychology, as well as licenses to practice traditional therapy. Some, however, do not. If you are a patient, it's important to do some research to understand what degrees, licenses and accolades your counselor has acquired, and what they all mean. Finding the right therapist or counselor may be a lengthy process, but it can be made worlds easier when you know what you are looking for before you begin. Reserve the right to be picky; your therapist or counselor should be an individual that you feel comfortable with, who respects you and works to earn your respect in turn. No amount of degrees or licenses should override your sense that someone isn't right for you, nor should a lack of appropriate credentials stop you from working with someone who seems like a good fit.

- Chapter 8 -

PHYSICAL HEALING
METHODS

MASSAGE

Massages aren't just about luxury and self-indulgence. A skilled massage therapist—especially one with empathic gifts—can do incredible work to heal discomfort, inflammation, stress injuries, and even some types of organ dysfunction. They can also address emotional issues, like stress, grief, anxiety, or chronic anger.

Training to become a massage therapist usually involves extensive study of human anatomy, allowing the masseuse to gain a thorough understanding of connective tissues, organ systems, and muscular function. Empaths have a competitive edge here, as they can often sense the root of other people's physical discomfort and see a clear pathway to relieving their tension or pain, even without extensive knowledge of anatomic systems.

As is the case with most of the healing arts listed in this text, empaths who choose to either receive or perform massage therapy are advised to strengthen their boundaries and use whatever means necessary—whether it is the creation of an energy shield, or wearing a protective crystal pendant during sessions—to protect themselves from emotional contagion during sessions. There are three primary reasons for this recommendation. First, many people fall into a relaxed and meditative state during a massage session, whether they intend to or not; this meditative energy is powerful, and can forge a deep connection between the therapist and the client on the table, one which is sometimes more intimate than either party desires. Secondly, effective massage can help to release deep-seated tensions, which are often linked to repressed memories or long-stifled emotions. When these issues are brought to the surface, difficult feelings, raw pain, and other typical reactions to trauma permeate the energy field between the client and masseuse; emotional contagion is a serious risk here.

Finally, since many empaths emit warm and caring energy to all people, regardless of the level of intimacy or attraction that exists between them, some clients may misinterpret the meaning of their kind attitude and sensuous touch as genuine romantic or sexual interest. Empaths who work as massage therapists may receive fairly frequent advances, sometimes from clients who genuinely believe the empath is coming on to them, or sometimes from clients who want to take advantage of them or feel entitled to sexual gratification. Many massage therapists work in private spaces, so this may be a real risk for any empath who is still processing a sexually-based trauma or history of personal violation.

ACUPRESSURE

Acupressure is similar to massage but incorporates many of the healing theories of acupuncture, a traditional Chinese method of alternative treatment (which is detailed later in this chapter). Rather than running the hands over the body in a soothing way, targeting muscle groups, tendons, and joints, acupressure targets specific points in the body, and exerts intense, focused pressure upon them, often for several minutes at a time, in order to trigger tension release and restore energy flow throughout the body. Typically, the pressure is applied through just one or two fingertips, pressing deeply into the flesh and moving in a restricted circular motion. This pressure is intended to signal the body's natural healing mechanisms and restore its internal regulatory systems.

Acupressure can be performed upon others, or upon oneself. Generally, multiple sessions are recommended to ensure lasting benefits. As compared to acupuncture, acupressure is much easier to learn and begin practicing, as it focuses of only eight primary pressure points in the body (whereas there are upwards of 350 points used in classical acupuncture theory) and is essentially risk free, so long as you only use as much force as can be applied through two fingers.

Empath healers may find some of the theories of acupressure seem natural and instinctive. Physical empaths, in particular, can pick up this skill quite quickly and develop incredible nuance in their appli cation, as they'll be able to sense which pressure points need the most attention in their patients, as well as which might trigger painful or uncomfortable sensations.

PHYSICAL THERAPY

Unlike most healing forms listed in this text, physical therapy is widely embraced by western medicine and is typically recommended by doctors as part of a post-treatment or long-term recovery process. Those who are ill or injured can benefit from regular physical therapy sessions, retraining their bodies to function optimally, and learning how to manage their pain without prescription drugs.

The goal of most physical therapy is rehabilitation through stretching and various forms of exercise. Physical therapy does not usually address holistic health concerns or explore the ways in which our emotions and mental states impact the function of our organs, muscles, and endocrine systems. Empaths may find that work in physical therapy provides them with many opportunities to provide care, support, and healing insight to those who are most in need, as patients are usually past the point wherein western medicine can offer them any further relief or treatment. They must take care, though, to shield themselves emotionally and physically from empathic contagion, as most of their patients will be in a significant amount of pain and potentially recovering from emotional trauma, as well.

YOGA

These days, many people think of yoga primarily as a form of exercise, but this ancient Indian practice was originally designed as a holistic healing method, promoting harmony between the heart, soul, body, and the divine elements. It is an amazingly versatile tool, accessible to the young and old, rich and poor, regardless of body size, physical fitness level, race or gender. For those who do not put much stock in metaphysical workings, it is still a wonderful way to enhance flexibility and physical balance, build muscle, purge toxins, relieve stress, reduce pain and inflammation, correct poor posture or misalignment issues, and prevent stress injuries. If you are able to embrace the spiritual side of yoga and incorporate meditation, mantras and chakra alignment, crystal healing, or other forms of spiritual or metaphysical energy work into your time on the mat, there is no end to what you might stand to gain from your practice. Yoga can simultaneously address physical, mental, and emotional health issues. It can be humbling and empowering, meditative and playful, awkward, and comfortable, all at once.

Some forms of yoga are slower, milder, calmer, and involve little to no physical exertion; other forms can be faster-paced, with difficult poses and complex sequences of movement. The latter can be extremely physically challenging, and will likely encourage toxin release through heavy sweat. All forms of yoga, no matter how strenuous or relaxing will involve a focus on mindful breathing, with inhalations and exhalations synchronized with specific movements. Any practice that incorporates pranayama will be particularly focused on harnessing the power of our breath, breathing mindfully, and using breath strategically to certain power postures.

Hatha yoga is a great place to start if you're feeling at all intimidated about dipping your toes into the rich, rewarding world of yoga. Hatha classes are highly instructional, leading students through some of the most basic and accessible poses with step by step guidance. A Hatha class isn't likely to get you sweating or to purge too many toxins, but it will help you to improve flexibility, balance, and focus, to reduce your stress levels, and encourage you to feel more comfortable and confident on a yoga mat. It's a wonderful introductory practice, but experienced yogis can also stand to gain a lot by returning to the basics in a Hatha class.

Iyengar yoga is a slow-paced practice that focuses on finding proper and sustainable alignment in every single pose. Teachers typically help their students to achieve ideal alignment despite their own physical limitations by providing props—blankets, blocks, straps, and so on—that help to keep their bodies in the right position. Though the classes move fairly slowly, you may be quite surprised at how exhausted you are by the end of one session, as the practice takes a great deal of physical tenacity and mental focus. Iyengar is a great choice for yogi's healing from an injury or suffering from chronic pain.

Restorative yoga is also a wonderful option for those with pain conditions or anyone in need of a rejuvenating experience. In these classes, most poses are built while lying down on the floor, using props when necessary, to allow yogis to experience deep stretches and realignment without any exertion or strain on the muscles. As in Iyengar, these poses are usually held for several minutes at a time, encouraging deep relaxation and tension release. Classes are usually more soothing and calming than energizing, and they are often offered later in the evenings by low light or candlelight, sometimes including aromatherapy, to help students transition into a restful mode at the end of a long workday or week. Most teachers of restorative and Iyengar yoga are prepared to offer special accommodations or instructions to students with injuries or health concerns.

Ashtanga and Bikram yoga classes may be ideal for yogi's who prefer a predictable routine that they can practice and perfect over time. Ashtanga is a challenging and faster-paced practice that follows the same exact series of postures in every single class. Bikram yoga also follows the same routine sequence in every class, but classes are held in artificially heated rooms to enhance flexibility and toxin release.

If you prefer more variety in your classes, you may instead choose Vinyasa yoga in place of Ashtanga, or a Hot Yoga class over a Bikram class. Vinyasa yoga classes work through a different series of postures in each session, and teachers frequently remind students that it is perfectly fine if they don't catch a pose or two, fall out of rhythm with the rest of the class, or have to bow out for a few minutes and rest in child's pose. Vinyasa moves fairly quickly, but the focus is on fluid, graceful movements connected to the rhythmic breath, rather than on achieving perfect alignment in each pose. Hot yoga classes are similar to Bikram classes; only they offer a varied sequence of poses in place of a standardized routine. Some yogis choose Hot Yoga over Bikram yoga consistently, as the founder of the Bikram style has attracted some controversy since the style was first popularized, and some find his teachings, leadership style, and business practices to involve questionable ethics.

Anusara is a relatively new introduction to the world of yoga, but quite a welcome one. This style is both physically and emotionally restorative, incorporating tantric philosophy to teach the universal principles of alignment. It proclaims that there is inherent goodness in each and every one of us, and uses postures in combination with mantras, affirmations, and other tools to encourage students to open their hearts and interact with the world through the lens of love, tolerance, and positivity. Anusara is an interdisciplinary style that requires full involvement of the physical, emotional, mental, and spiritual bodies. It is physically similar to the Vinyasa style but looks at the practice in a more holistic and spiritual way.

There are many other yoga traditions and styles, from Jivamukti or Kundalini yoga (which incorporate chakra alignment work and chanting of mantras) to naked rooftop yoga classes. Each style has its own unique set of benefits to offer students, and there is no reason why you should not incorporate multiple schools of thought into your own yoga practice.

Many people are intimidated by the face of yoga that they see in popular culture and social media, where the focus seems to be on complicated, acrobatic poses and a strangely materialistic, competitive, cult-like culture. Some yoga studios do indeed market a version of this ancient practice that is more focused on physical beauty than internal health or emotional well-being and promotes exclusivity over inclusivity, with very little attention drawn to the meditative or spiritual side of yoga. Even so, there are still plenty of studios and independent teachers that honor yoga as a healing art, respecting its oldest traditions and targeting the poses that offer the greatest emotional and physical benefits to their students, rather than those poses that look most impressive in an Instagram post. It is wise to try a few different teachers and studios that offer varied forms of yoga before settling into a routine so that you can find a practice that truly serves you. If you are unable to find a teacher who fulfills your needs, it may be time to consider enrolling in a teacher training course and becoming the kind of teacher you wish you'd been able to learn from! These days, yoga classes can be held in established studios, in homes, in public places, in the great outdoors, and even on the internet, so as a certified teacher, you can impact as few or as many lives as your ambition and drive will allow you to.

ENERGY HEALING

There are many different forms of energy healing, and we'll only touch on some of the most popular forms in this text. Energy healing works to treat the individual's physical, emotional, mental and spiritual bodies all as one, respecting each as interconnected entities that are all impacted by one another, and which should not be compartmentalized or treated separately. It is most effective when all parties involved—both the healer and the recipient of healing energy—are willing to believe and invest emotional energy into the process. Here, we'll detail two of the most well-known forms of energy healing: Reiki and Chakra work. Bear in mind, though, that there are many alternatives to these specific traditions, and endless possibilities if you should choose to combine two or more energy healing strategies.

REIKI

Reiki is an ancient Japanese tradition of energy healing. It works to channel "ki," which is a flowing, energetic life force, through the three "tandens," or centers of energy, in our bodies. The first tanden is found in crown or forehead (in the same place as the third eye chakra, detailed further in the next section of this chapter) and connects us to heavenly energy; the second is the heart tanden, located in the center of the chest, which connects us to human energy, or emotional energy; the third, and most vital of the three, is referred to as "hara," found in the gut, below the belly button, and is the source of both earth energy and "Original energy." Original energy is a term that describes what makes you the person you are: your soul, your purpose, your life path, your essence, and your destiny.

Ki is described as a fluid, everchanging substance that flows in and out of our metaphysical bodies; we do not maintain a fixed amount of ki throughout our lives, but rather, the amount we harness fluctuates in relation to the way we treat ourselves and the manner in which we interact with the world around us. When ki is low, our life force is weakened, and we are more susceptible to illness, discomfort, burnout, emotional dissociation or anguish, and anxiety. When a person has a high level of ki, they are happier, healthier, more energized, motivated, and ready to thrive. Like oxygen, there is an unlimited amount of ki available in our world; the purpose of Reiki is to make sure the body is breathing it in deeply enough to experience all its beneficial effects. Since there is no limit to the amount of ki available for channeling, Reiki is a wonderful healing tool for empaths who are especially susceptible to energy depletion, because it allows the healer to channel energy from the universe, rather than drawing energy from their own metaphysical bodies. There is also a low risk for emotional contagion in an attunement session, as the Reiki master channels ki directly from God; like an empty glass vessel transporting water, the master's personality and current mood do not impact the nature of the spiritual energy flowing into the receiver.

Reiki attunement is not only used for healing physical discomfort; it is also used to combat stress and promote relaxation on both physical and metaphysical levels. Reiki is also a tool used to encourage spiritual growth. It is often spoken of as a gift from God. However, Reiki is not associated with any particular religious dogma. This makes it accessible to people from all cultures and faiths. It can only help, and it can never cause harm.

Compared to some other forms of energy healing, such as Chakra cleansing work, Reiki is an easily accessible healing style to receive as treatment and learn to perform yourself. Anyone can become a Reiki healer—all they really need to get started is initiation, or purposeful transfer of healing energy, from an established Reiki master. This can take place during a healing session, and it isn't a very time-consuming process. After one single attunement and teacher-to-student energy transfer, you will be ready to start healing others with your own ki energy.

Reiki is a natural and safe healing practice, one that poses no potential health risk at all to those who receive attunements. To the casual observer, it may simply look like a gentler, low-contact, and low-pressure version of a massage. The master uses what is called "palm healing" or "hands-on healing" to transfer and balance energy within the receiver's body. The practice is generally quiet and soothing. It can be used in combination with other forms of energy healing (crystal work, meditation, soul retrieval, and more) to optimize and personalize the recipient's healing experience.

If you're not sure whether or not Reiki should be a part of your healing practice, the best way to learn more is to contact a Reiki master and sign up for an attunement. Reiki is something that has to be experienced in order to be fully understood; words fail to describe its power for healing and growth.

CHAKRA CLEANSING AND ALIGNMENT

Chakra work has several similarities to Reiki; though this healing tradition originated in India rather than Japan, it is entirely possible that both practices evolved from a unified source of truth, translated through different cultures and languages.

In Chakra's work, "kundalini" is the vital energy that vibrates through all living, celestial, and metaphysical bodies. It is the life force that drives us and connects us all; it is the energy that flows through all of the chakras in our bodies, rooting us to the earth while simultaneously linking us to the divine. Some visualize kundalini as a physically ineffable spiritual energy; others picture it as a bright, vibrant light in liquid form that can flow through our chakras most efficiently when they are well aligned and balanced. Kundalini is sometimes characterized as "serpent power," coiled around the root chakra, or as the "sleeping goddess" within who is awakened when the chakras are all aligned and channeling energy in concert.

The word "chakra" means "wheel" in ancient Sanskrit, so each of the seven chakras is depicted as a wheel made of spinning energy, like a whirlpool, inside the body, found at various points along the spinal column. Each chakra is connected to different body parts and organ systems; each has its own emotional and mental health component; each is related to a different element, color, symbol, and resonating sonic frequency. People typically talk about chakras falling out of balance, but this term is often an overgeneralization. Chakras can also be clogged, or too open; they can be reversed, spinning energy in the "wrong" direction, as compared to the others housed in the same body; they can be dormant, or overactive. Each type of dysfunction presents through different symptoms or manifestations. It's also important to remember that the chakras are meant to function as a whole system, so there are no playing favorites with them; focusing on one chakra to the detriment of others will only encourage further imbalance, discomfort, and dysfunction.

Though chakra work is an ancient healing art, with roots deeper in history than our modern understandings of anatomy and medicine, it may appeal even to those who are the most skeptic of the metaphysical, because the seven chakras are a shockingly accurate reflection of our endocrine systems. An endocrine system is a group of glands that control hormone release within our bodies, and hormones dictate just about every aspect of our lives, from our sleeping and eating habits to our moods and energy levels.

Healing work for any of the seven chakras is often a holistic effort. It may involve recommendations of dietary changes, specific types of movement (sexual activity, for example, or dance), altered sleep habits, particular yoga poses, lifestyle changes, talk therapy, massage, or another form of energy healing. These recommendations may sometimes seem outlandish, such as the suggestion to wear more of a certain color—red for the root chakra, green for the heart chakra, and so on—to restore balance, or to use specific crystals to channel energy to the chakras that need attention. Remember to keep an open mind as a patient, student, or practitioner of chakra alignment work. It would be a shame to miss a healing opportunity for the sake of honoring skepticism, doubt, or disbelief.

All chakras are equally important in healing work, but empaths especially may wish to focus on balancing their solar plexus chakra, which is found in the stomach. The solar plexus chakra is where we house our emotions, or egos, our sense of self-esteem and confidence in our abilities. Most empaths struggle to keep this chakra properly energized throughout their lives, as they have far more emotions to process than the average individual, and they often pour so much energy into others that they never manage to build a stable sense of self.

There are seven major chakras, which are most commonly referenced in energy healing work, but if you wish to dive deep into this practice, you might want to study the minor chakras as well, of which there are an additional five. The twelve-chakra system may be of special interest to geomantic empaths, as it focuses on grounding the balanced body and connecting it to the earth.

SOUND HEALING

Sound healing is also sometimes referred to as "vibrational medicine." It employs various sonic tools, including the human voice, tuning forks, Tibetan singing bowls, digeridoos, gongs, and others, to target specific vibrational frequencies that will encourage relaxation, pain relief, and healing.

Sound is a physical element; if you've ever been to a rock concert and felt the bassline thrumming through the floor, into your feet, legs, gut, and chest, then you know how certain notes and volumes can impact a person's physical and emotional body immediately. We also feel sonic vibrations inside our bodies whenever we speak or sing, though most of us have grown so accustomed to these feelings that we've learned to ignore them. Through sound healing, we can grow to be more mindful of these sensations, and eventually come to use them in strategic manners to impact our energy levels, psychological patterns, and pain management routines.

Music and other forms of sound can impact brain function, altering our moods, helping us to wake up or fall asleep, providing energy or promoting tension release. The theory of sound healing has primarily gained popularity in the last few decades, but threads of this theory can be traced back to a number of ancient healing traditions. In Chakra's work, for example, each energy center in the body corresponds to a particular mantra sound, which patients are often encouraged to chant or sing during their healing sessions in order to channel energetic vibrations to certain areas of the body. The employment of music for healing purposes was also popular in Native American and ancient Egyptian healing traditions.

Empaths may choose to use sound healing in one-on-one meetings with clients, in group sessions, or within the frame of a multidisciplinary healing environment. Sound healers can work with shamans, yoga instructors, Reiki masters, or massage therapists to enhance their efficacy in healing; or, alternatively, they might choose to simply create music with healing vibrations that can be performed, recorded, and enjoyed by believers and non-believers alike.

ACUPUNCTURE

Acupuncture is an alternative medicinal practice that originated in China thousands of years ago and is still popularly used today throughout the world. It is a practice in which extremely thin needles are pushed into the skin at various points throughout the body. The needles are usually only inserted to reach a depth of about 1-2 millimeters below the skin's surface, but in some cases, they can go several inches deep. The process is typically not painful, though; the points at which the needles are inserted are acupoints, just like those targeted in acupressure, and when they are gently prodded with these hair-thin needles, they help to release tensions, purge toxins from the body, promote healing and relaxation. Many patients are lulled to sleep in acupuncture sessions; the most intense level of pain they might experience is similar to that of a deep-tissue massage, and the pain is typically fleeting.

Acupuncture theory has some similarities to that of Reiki and Chakra alignment; it focuses on restoring balance and function of vital energy called "qi" which can cause emotional and physical health problems if clogged, imbalanced, or otherwise dysfunctional. Qi should flow freely from the internal organs to the surface layer organs, like the skin, along lines called "meridians." In acupuncture, needles are usually placed along the meridian lines in order to reach the deeper organs connected to them.

Empaths are well-suited to this healing art, primarily because the ability to determine where acupuncture needles are placed often rests on the practitioner's ability to read a patient's energy field. Some acupuncturists determine the placement of needles in a method that is similar to Reiki, hovering their hands over the body or placing them gently upon the skin, and waiting for disturbances in the patient's energy field to physically trip them up or alert them in some other way (visually, sonically, or perhaps even triggering a physical sensation within the practitioner's body). However, this is not a practice that can be winged or performed on the fly; most countries in the world require acupuncturists to acquire licenses from regulatory boards before seeing their own patients, a process which involves thousands of hours of training and education.

HOMEOPATHY

Homeopathy is an alternative to traditional western medicine. Established in the late 1700s, its theories rest upon the notion that our bodies have the ability to heal themselves without much intervention on our part, and that in order to encourage specific forms of healing, we can introduce extremely small amounts of substances that would serve to promote illness in larger quantities. This theory is similar to that of vaccines: by introducing a minuscule, heavily distilled amount of unwelcome substance to the body, we can trigger the body's natural autoimmune responses.

There is a great deal of skepticism as to the effectiveness of homeopathic remedies within the world of western medicine, but in some cases, homeopathy has proven itself to be an effectual element in alternative healing journeys. Empaths may be particularly capable in this field, as the determination of which diluted substances should be prescribed to any patient rests heavily upon acquiring and evaluating detailed information about the patient's life—likes, dislikes, disposition, diet, emotional circumstances, past illnesses and injuries, and aspects of their daily routine.

There are homeopathic remedies available to treat a vast array of illnesses and emotional upsets, from the common cold to a spell of grief. Homeopathy can be combined with any number of other alternative medicine theories to promote holistic healing and restore internal balance.

NATUROPATHY

You might think of naturopathy as an umbrella term, one which can encompass various forms of alternative healing. The basic premise of naturopathy is that healing from all sorts of maladies and injuries can be accomplished without the use of modern drugs or invasive surgeries. Naturopaths design healing regimens that include exercise, dietary changes, massage, and sometimes even emotionally based recommendations (for instance, someone suffering from an ulcer might be advised to change their career or end a relationship that is causing them stress).

Empaths can make wonderful naturopaths because they are able to see both minor details and the big picture. They will be able to help their patients make changes that are not only necessary and beneficial, but also sustainable because they'll be able to understand the patient's individual capabilities and challenges, strengths, and weaknesses, and so on. The goal of naturopathy isn't short-term healing; it aims to create lasting lifestyle changes that will ensure a balance between the physical and emotional bodies and allow both to function optimally throughout a patient's life. Naturopaths often help to connect their patients with experts in various fields of alternative medicine, such as acupuncturists or homeopaths. Empathic naturopaths can be particularly adept in this area, as they'll be able to predict which practitioners will be a good fit for their patients, and help to foster connections between them, as well as between healers who might work well together.

AYURVEDA

Ayurveda is one of the oldest holistic healing traditions in the world. This Hindu practice promotes good health through very specific recommendations of when and what to eat, how much to sleep, how to exercise, and even how to breathe. It looks at the mind, body, and soul as inextricably linked, and believes that good health can only be achieved by finding a balance between all three of these elements. It is generally considered a preventative health measure, rather than a healing strategy. Most practitioners would not recommend it as a cure for cancer, but some believe it can help to prevent or delay the onset of diseases.

Ayurveda is Sanskrit for "the science of life." As such, it is a fairly complex school of thought which requires extensive study to grasp fully. It makes some generalized recommendations, such as the consumption of whole, unprocessed foods and frequent movement of the body—but

Ayurveda also recognizes that each individual is unique, and their needs will vary based on circumstances. A practitioner will typically make a detailed evaluation of a patient's physical, mental, and spiritual health before offering any prescribed treatments or lifestyle changes.

Empaths may find the study and practice of Ayurvedic theory to be particularly rewarding, as it offers them the ability to connect with patients on multiple levels and design unique healing plans for each client.

Chapter 9

MENTAL AND SPIRITUAL
HEALING METHODS

GROUNDING

Grounding, like meditation, is one of the easiest and most accessible healing methods available to those with limited financial resources. It is a wonderful option for those who are short on time and need to maintain emotional balance and energy levels in the face of intense stressors.

All one needs for grounding is a willingness to spend some time outdoors, connecting to nature physically through skin contact. The most basic form of grounding is to walk, or stand, barefoot on natural earth, be it a patch of grass, a sandy shoreline, or a rocky cliffside. Some choose to incorporate yoga into their grounding practice, standing in Mountain Pose (Tadasana), sitting in any variation of Lotus Pose (Padmasana), or lying down in Corpse Pose (Shavasana) to connect with the earth. With skin contact established, take some time to practice mindful breathing; taste the air around you; check in with every physical and emotional sensation currently being held in your body, and accept them for what they are.

Now close your eyes, and check-in with the ground beneath you. How does it feel? Warm or cool? Moist or dry? Smooth or rough? As you breathe naturally, consider all the elements that led this ground to feel exactly as it does beneath your feet. Is it shaped by the winds and waters around it? Does it bask in the sun's light and soak up all its energy, or does it take respite in the shade of a nearby tree? Think of all the myriad ways this particular piece of earth is at one with all the elements surrounding it.

Now, with your eyes still closed and your breathing steady, picture yourself—your aura, your energy, your soul's entire being—as another one of these natural elements, like air, or water, or the warmth of the sun. Picture your energy flowing down into the ground like water into a well, and picture the energy of the earth rising up and flowing through your body, in turn. Imagine yourself growing roots like a tree, feeding off the earth's energy and replenishing that energy with gratitude. Recognize that you are connecting to the earth, and impacting it, shaping it, just as the wind and rain and sun do. This experience should be empowering and humbling, all at once; it should help you to feel that you are a part of something much larger and greater than yourself, but also that you are a vital component of the universe's energy.

Regular grounding is recommended for anyone who suffers from chronic imbalance or disturbance of the root chakra, as it will work to reinforce the notion that the universe will hold you up, if you should fall, and remind you that no matter what happens with your family, friends, co-workers or lovers, you belong; you are worthy; you are impactful; and you are enough, just as you are. Those who are feeling particularly drained or depleted may stand to gain the most from grounding in full, direct sunlight, during the early afternoon hours when the ground has had adequate time to soak up the sun's energy and warmth.

CRYSTAL HEALING

Crystals can be incorporated into almost any type of energy healing practice. They can also do powerful work on their own, either when worn or placed strategically in crystal grids. Each type of crystal possesses its own unique set of metaphysical properties; some are recommended for deflecting negative energies, while others absorb or nullify them; some may enhance mental clarity or promote self-confidence; some might be particularly useful in trauma recovery or certain types of pain management. Specific stones are related to each of the seven chakras to target health concerns and correct misalignment.

Here is a list of crystals that are particularly recommended for empaths, and the reasons why they might be useful to you. There are many, many more that you may find resonate with your individual needs.

- Hematite – Soothes and helps you to stay centered; shields against energy depletion

- Apache Gold – also called "healer's gold," this stone helps to strengthen boundaries and encourage clear, honest communication

- Labradorite – Enhances intuition, promotes emotional stability and creativity

- Malachite (polished only) – Clears emotional clogs, promotes the release of tension and negative emotions, neutralizes negative energies from technology sources

- Black tourmaline – Deflects negative energies and channels them into the earth for transformation; protective stone, especially recommended for geomantic empaths

- Carnelian – Promotes physical healing, targeting metabolic function and circulation; empowers and restores self-confidence, as well as a sense of capability

- Citrine – Enhances the function of the solar plexus chakra and the digestive organs; purges emotional blockages and shields against negativity.

- Amethyst – Strengthens intuition, cleanses the aura, and promotes harmony and peace.

Whatever crystals you choose to wear or use in your energy healing practice, be mindful of the fact that crystals need to cleansed regularly. This can be done through smudging, bathing your crystals in the light of a full moon, or even burying them underground overnight before retrieving them. Furthermore, be conscious of the properties of any crystals you choose to use in concert; if their energies work in opposing directions, they may end up nullifying each other's powers.

SHAMANIC HEALING

Shamans are spiritual beings who can translate the messages of the divine for acceptance in the human realm, and vice versa. The tradition of shamanism is ancient and derived primarily from indigenous groups, but there is a growing wave of neo-shamanism, in which modern practitioners are able to design their own spiritual practices, incorporating some ancient traditions while weaving in some of their own inventions.

Shamans are religious leaders who may use their power to heal, communicate with non-human spirits, and even cross back and forth over the line between this world and the afterlife. They are able to guide individuals through intense spiritual journeys that involve ritualistic practices, and sometimes the use of hallucinogenic substances.

A shaman can help to guide your spirit on a number of journeys, including, but not limited to:

- **Soul Retrieval** – A process in which is very similar to the process of reconnecting with your core identity or authentic self as outlined in chapter 4, but achieved through spiritual rituals rather than practical measures. This journey is focused on reclaiming the part of the soul that is lost through traumas in early life and returning to a place of fulfillment.

- **Cutting off ties** – This is similar to the Cord Cutting ceremony referenced in chapter 7, however it can be used to release you from the grip of addictions or toxic behavioral patterns, as well as interpersonal relationships.

- **Past life regression** – This journey is never to be taken lightly and should not be fulfilled simply to satisfy curiosity. A past life may be visited in order to heal from traumas that took place before your lifetime, or to uncover hidden truths from the past that still inform your current identity.

- **Journeying** – A shaman may escort you on a journey into the spirit world, to achieve various forms of enlightenment and personal growth.

Chapter 10

PRIORITIZING SELF-CARE

Hopefully, by this point, you've been able to select a few healing methods that appeal to your sensibilities. With your empathic gifts thriving, there is no limit to what you might achieve once you make the decision to chase your dreams and spread your healing light.

Still, no matter how far you've come in this journey, it is never a bad time to remember to put yourself first. As a healer, you'll be surrounded by people whose needs will seem more urgent, more important, more vital, than your own. In these situations, your compassionate nature will work against your better judgment, and the temptation to push yourself beyond your own limits may be overpowering.

One great way to protect against this is to establish your self-care routine and engrain it into your schedule and your relationships *before* you dive into healing work. You might even make a list of your self-care needs and review it regularly, like a check-list, to ensure you are continually respecting your own limits and putting yourself first.

Here are some common self-care needs of empaths to inspire you. These items may not all resonate with you, and you might find you have plenty of needs that aren't listed. Draw up a list for yourself, and make it as long or as short as you like. Remember, no one can ever know you as well as you know yourself, and no one else can define how much self-care or self-love you deserve to shower yourself with.

- Space for honest and open emotive expression – We empaths feel things very deeply. If we are immersed in an environment where our emotions aren't welcome—where tears or anguish need to be hidden away—we eventually learn to doubt ourselves and the validity of our emotional responses. Give yourself permission to back away from relationships or environments that consistently put you in the position of having to swallow, mitigate, or lie about your feelings. Work to build a support system of people who also value emotional authenticity and are not frightened by deep, intense feelings. Trust me; they're out there!

- Alone time – Even if your friends and colleagues are the loveliest of people, as an empath, you may feel the urge to hide from the world every once in a while. This is perfectly natural and nothing to be ashamed of. In fact, you might grow to feel a lot more positive about these reclusive spells if you schedule them regularly and plan them out, rather than waiting until you feel so overwhelmed by life that you simply cannot convince yourself to leave your bedroom. Alone time can be restorative, productive, and fun, so long as you save yourself enough energy to be able to enjoy it.

- Adequate rest – Empaths may have extraordinary gifts, but we are still human, and therefore, we need to make sure we get enough sleep in order to function. You may also need to schedule some downtime for yourself that is separate from your sleep schedule or your alone time—time that is unscheduled, devoid of stressors or sources of anxiety, with which you can do whatever you choose. Read a book, reorganize your sock drawer, bake some cookies, or go for a walk with a friend. These activities can be restorative, just like a good night's sleep.

- A health-focused diet – Since so many of us have trouble with our solar plexus chakra and digestive organs, it can be lifechanging to place some firm boundaries around your eating habits. Others will constantly pressure you to abandon these, primarily because your dedication to healthy eating will make them feel guilty for eating haphazardly and irresponsibly. Don't let others sway your decision to give your body the fuel that it needs. It's never worth it to suffer from indigestion, stomach cramps, or emotional turmoil, just to make someone else feel better about their own dietary choices.

- Physical comforts – Others might call you needy, picky, high-maintenance. So what? As an empath, you are more sensitive than most to changes in temperature, itchy or uncomfortable synthetic fabrics, lights, sounds, and scents. Maybe what you really need to feel comfortable is a full outfit made of organic cotton, a thermostat set at precisely 71 degrees, natural sunlight, the scent of lavender essential oils, and some music that is quiet—but not too quiet. Find time and space wherein you can feel entitled to all the things that make you comfortable. Revel in it. You only get one life. Why spend it being uncomfortable, just to avoid judgment from other people?

- Fairness and reciprocity – We all have relationships in our lives that feel a little unbalanced at times. One thing that empaths tend to forget, though, is that if we fill our lives up with these kinds of relationships, we don't leave any room for the kinds of relationships we *do* want. A great way to care for yourself and stop toxic emotions like resentment from flourishing inside you is to address injustices or one-sided relationship behaviors immediately before they can spin out of control. If you never allow someone to take advantage of your kindness, then you never have to deal with feeling resentful down the line. Work to surround yourself with people and institutions that also value fairness and reciprocity. When you stumble into those that don't, there's no reason to waste your energy in fighting them; just walk away, and channel your energies into finding a better place to be.

- Authenticity and sustainability – Empaths thrive best when they build lives for themselves that are centered around honesty, real connection, and forethought. Lies and inefficient systems stick out to us like sore thumbs, and while most people can shrug these things off, we often find them impossible to ignore or tolerate. As such, you may derive a great deal of peace of mind by investing in authenticity and sustainability as a lifestyle. Though it may be a difficult transition at first, choose to spend your money on items that are designed to last, rather than that which is cheap and disposable. Tailor your social media consumption to only let in authentic images and messages. Remove any relationships from your life that are built upon dishonesty. Make plans for your home, your career, your relationships, and your body that can evolve into the long-term. Find your own way to contribute to environmental sustainability, whether it's switching to an electric car, planting more trees in your own backyard, or starting up a recycling initiative in your office.

Whatever you choose to incorporate into your self-care routine, remember to treat it as a priority—not the last thing on your to-do list, which is likely to get edged off when anything unexpected comes up. When you set aside regular time to care for and appreciate yourself, you'll be able to function at an elevated level; more importantly, your ability to connect with others empathically will be strengthened and enhanced by your own self-love.

CONCLUSION

Thank you for making it through to the end of *Empath Healing: The Empath's Survival Guide. Simple And Effective Practices To Become An Energy Healer And Develop Your Mystic Consciousness.* Let's hope it was informative and able to provide you with all of the tools you need to achieve your goals, whatever they may be.

The next step is to start experimenting with various healing methods in order to find one—or several, if you're lucky—that address your needs. It is always advisable to experience any healing practice from the standpoint of a patient, client, or student before jumping into a training program or offering yourself as a healer.

It is also wise to focus on connecting with as many other empaths and alternative healers as you can find, both socially and professionally. There may not be many fellow empaths in your immediate social or professional circles, but I assure you, like-minded spirits are out there, and they are eager to receive and connect with you! Browse online forums, podcasts, and social media platforms; seek out retreats, or find an inclusive spiritual organization in your area; yoga classes attract empaths like moths to a flame. It may take some effort, but once you start to keep an eye out for fellow empaths, you may be pleasantly surprised to find that we are everywhere, and we all want to support your journey to become a healer.

When empaths come together, their combined strength is multiplied exponentially. Though we are gaining recognition in the fields of psychology and science, we still are a minority in the world. We must support each other, empower each other, share our personal stories, and teach each other, to ensure that the light of empathy continues to spread and grow brighter with every passing year.

Finally, if you found this book useful in any way, a review on Amazon is always appreciated! Spread your light and healing energy by ensuring this book finds its way to as many fellow empaths as possible.